THE ULTIMA MEDITERRANEAN DIET COOKBOOK FOR BEGINNERS (FULL COLOR VERSION)

1500 Days Of Luscious, Healthy, And Vibrant Recipes To Fall In Love With Home Cooking, Exercise, And Building Healthy Habits.

RHONDA M. REEVES

Table of Contents

The Standard American Diet (SAD) is characterized by a high intake of processed foods, added sugars, saturated and trans fats, and refined grains, and a low intake of fruits, vegetables, and whole grains. This dietary pattern is often associated with a high risk of chronic diseases such as obesity, heart disease, type 2 diabetes, and certain types of cancer.

High in added sugars and refined carbohydrates: The Standard American Diet is high in added sugars, which are found in many processed foods and sweetened beverages. This can lead to weight gain, insulin resistance, and an increased risk of type 2 diabetes. Refined carbohydrates, such as white bread and pasta, are also commonly consumed in the SAD, which can cause spikes in blood sugar and contribute to obesity and diabetes.

Low in fruits and vegetables: Fruits and vegetables are important sources of vitamins, minerals, and antioxidants. However, the Standard American Diet is typically low in these foods, which can lead to deficiencies in essential nutrients and an increased risk of chronic diseases.

High in saturated and trans fats: The Standard American Diet is high in saturated and trans fats, which are found in many processed foods, fast foods, and baked goods. These types of fats have been linked to an increased risk of heart disease, stroke, and certain types of cancer.

Low in fiber: The Standard American Diet is often low in fiber, which is essential for maintaining a healthy gut, preventing constipation, and reducing the risk of chronic diseases such as heart disease and type 2 diabetes.

High in sodium: The Standard American Diet is high in sodium, which can contribute to high blood pressure and an increased risk of heart disease. Many processed foods, fast foods, and restaurant meals are high in sodium, and the average American consumes more than the recommended daily limit.

the Standard American Diet is associated with a high risk of chronic diseases and poor health outcomes, and is in contrast to the Mediterranean diet which is considered healthy and balanced. It is important to adopt a healthy eating pattern that includes a variety of nutrient-dense foods and limits processed foods and added sugars.

Chapter 1
Basics of Mediterranean Diet

Eat Like a Mediterranean

Eating like a Mediterranean involves incorporating traditional Mediterranean foods and dietary patterns into your daily routine. Here are some tips on how to eat like a Mediterranean:

Emphasize plant-based foods: Fruits, vegetables, whole grains, legumes, and nuts are staples of the Mediterranean diet and should make up the majority of your daily intake. Try to eat at least five servings of fruits and vegetables per day.

Include healthy fats: The Mediterranean diet is rich in healthy fats, such as olive oil, avocado, and nuts. Use olive oil as your primary source of fat for cooking and dressings, and try to include at least a handful of nuts in your diet every day.

Eat fish and seafood regularly: Fish and seafood are an important source of lean protein and omega-3 fatty acids in the Mediterranean diet. Aim to eat fish at least twice a week, and try to include a variety of different types of fish and seafood.

Limit red meat and processed foods: The Mediterranean diet is low in red meat and processed foods, which are typically high in saturated fat and added sugars. Try to limit your consumption of red meat and processed foods, and opt for lean protein sources such as fish and poultry instead.

Enjoy meals with friends and family: In Mediterranean cultures, meals are often enjoyed with friends and family, and are seen as a time for socialization and relaxation. Try to incorporate this aspect of Mediterranean culture into your own meals by eating with others and savoring your food.

Add herbs and spices: Mediterranean cuisine is known for its use of herbs and spices, which not only add flavor but also provide health benefits. Try to use herbs and spices to flavor your food instead of salt or sugar.

Drink in moderation: moderate consumption of red wine is considered healthy in the Mediterranean diet, but it's important to consume it in moderation. Avoid drinking to excess and be mindful of your overall alcohol consumption.

Incorporate physical activity: Mediterranean people are known to be active, and physical activity is an essential part of their lifestyle. Incorporate regular physical activity, such as walking, cycling, or swimming, into your daily routine.

Live Like a Mediterranean

Living like a Mediterranean involves incorporating the lifestyle and cultural practices of Mediterranean people into your daily routine. Here are some tips on how to live like a Mediterranean:

Embrace simplicity: Mediterranean cultures value simplicity and focus on the essentials in life. Try to simplify your life by getting rid of unnecessary possessions and focusing on what truly matters.

Spend time outdoors: Mediterranean people spend a lot of time outdoors, whether it's working in the fields, going for a walk, or simply enjoying the sunshine. Try to spend more time outdoors, whether it's going for a walk, hiking, or gardening.

Prioritize social connections: Mediterranean cultures place a high value on social connections, and people often gather with friends and family to share meals and enjoy each other's company. Try to spend more time with friends and family, and make an effort to strengthen your social connections.

Embrace relaxation: Mediterranean cultures prioritize relaxation and leisure time. Try to incorporate more leisure activities into your daily routine, such as reading, painting, or taking a relaxing bath.

Practice mindfulness: Mediterranean cultures place a high value on mindfulness and living in the present moment. Try to practice mindfulness by paying attention to your thoughts and emotions, and focus on the present moment.

Incorporate physical activity: Mediterranean people are known to be active, and physical activity is an essential part of their lifestyle. Incorporate regular physical activity, such as walking, cycling, or swimming, into your daily routine.

Take care of your mental health: Mediterranean people place a high value on mental health, and they often seek professional help if they need it. Take care of your mental health by prioritizing self-care and seeking professional

help if needed.

Enjoying food: Mediterranean people take their time when it comes to eating, they savor their food and enjoy it while sharing it with others. Try to eat slowly and savor your food, and enjoy meals with friends and family.

By following these tips, you can start to live like a Mediterranean and enjoy the many benefits of this lifestyle. It's important to remember that, like any culture, the Mediterranean way of life is diverse, and it's hard to generalize it. Therefore, you can pick and choose the elements that resonate with you and incorporate them into your daily routine.

The Mediterranean Pyramid

The Mediterranean Diet Pyramid is a visual representation of the traditional dietary patterns of the Mediterranean region, which is characterized by a high intake of fruits, vegetables, whole grains, legumes, and nuts, moderate intake of fish and poultry, and low intake of red meat and dairy products.

At the base of the pyramid are fruits, vegetables, and whole grains, which are the foundation of the Mediterranean Diet and should be consumed in the greatest quantity. These foods are rich in vitamins, minerals, and antioxidants, and have been shown to lower the risk of chronic diseases such as heart disease and cancer.

Next, the pyramid includes legumes and nuts, which are good sources of protein and healthy fats. These foods are also high in fiber and have been linked to lower cholesterol levels and a reduced risk of heart disease.

On the next level of the pyramid are fish and poultry, which are recommended to be consumed in moderate amounts. These foods are lean sources of protein and are rich in omega-3 fatty acids, which have been shown to have numerous health benefits, including reducing inflammation and improving heart health.

The top level of the pyramid includes red meat and dairy products, which are recommended to be consumed in

Fruits · Vegetables · Whole Grains
Bread · Pasta · Rice · Olive Oil

EVERY MAIN MEAL

Cheese · Yogurt
Nuts · Wine

DAILY

Fish · Eggs
Poultry · Legumes

WEEKLY

MONTHLY

Meat

small amounts. These foods are high in saturated fat and cholesterol, and have been linked to an increased risk of heart disease and certain cancers.

Finally, the Mediterranean Diet Pyramid also includes a moderate intake of wine, which is typically consumed with meals and in moderation.

A Holistic Approach

NUTRITION ON A MEDITERRANEAN DIET

The Mediterranean diet is characterized by a high intake of fruits, vegetables, whole grains, legumes, and nuts, a moderate intake of fish and seafood, and a low intake of red meat and processed foods. This dietary pattern is rich in essential nutrients and has been associated with a lower risk of chronic diseases such as heart disease, type 2 diabetes, and certain types of cancer.

High in antioxidants: Fruits and vegetables are rich in antioxidants, which can help protect the body against damage from free radicals. These foods are also rich in vitamins and minerals, such as vitamin C, vitamin K, and potassium.

High in fiber: Whole grains, legumes, and fruits and vegetables are rich in fiber, which can help promote healthy digestion and reduce the risk of chronic diseases such as heart disease and type 2 diabetes.

Good source of omega-3 fatty acids: Fish and seafood are rich in omega-3 fatty acids, which are essential for heart health and can help reduce inflammation throughout the body.

Good source of monounsaturated fats: The Mediterranean diet is rich in monounsaturated fats, such as olive oil, which can help reduce the risk of heart disease.

Low in saturated fats: The Mediterranean diet is low in saturated fats, which are typically found in red meat and processed foods. This can help reduce the risk of heart disease and stroke.

Low in sodium: The Mediterranean diet is low in sodium, which can help lower blood pressure and reduce the risk of heart disease.

Low in added sugars: The Mediterranean diet is low in added sugars, which are typically found in processed foods and sweetened beverages. This can help reduce the risk of obesity and type 2 diabetes.

The Mediterranean diet is a well-balanced and nutritious diet that provides essential nutrients and can help reduce the risk of chronic diseases. It is important to note that Mediterranean diet is a pattern of eating and not a set of rigid rule, so it's not necessary to stick to it 100% but rather to follow the principles of it.

EXERCISE ON A MEDITERRANEAN LIFESTYLE

Exercise is an important aspect of the Mediterranean lifestyle and is closely linked to the overall health and well-being of Mediterranean people. Regular physical activity is an essential part of the Mediterranean way of life, and people often engage in activities such as walking, cycling, swimming, and gardening.

Improves cardiovascular health: Regular physical activity can help improve cardiovascular health by strengthening the heart and reducing the risk of heart disease.

Helps to maintain a healthy weight: Exercise can help to burn calories and maintain a healthy weight, which can reduce the risk of obesity and associated health problems.

Reduces the risk of chronic diseases: Regular physical activity can help reduce the risk of chronic diseases such as type 2 diabetes, heart disease, and certain types of cancer.

Improves mental health: Exercise can help improve mental health by reducing stress, anxiety, and depression.

Promotes relaxation: Exercise can also promote relaxation by releasing endorphins, also known as "feel-good" chemicals in the brain.

Improves overall quality of life: Regular physical activity can help improve overall quality of life by increasing energy levels, strengthening bones and muscles, and improving sleep.

Enhances social connections: Exercise can also be a great way to connect with others and form social connections. Many Mediterranean people enjoy physical activities such as hiking, dancing, and playing sports with friends and family.

It is important to note that the Mediterranean lifestyle promotes a moderate level of physical activity and not necessarily intense or competitive sports, it's more about integrating daily activity into one's life. Therefore, it's important to find physical activities that you enjoy and that fit into your daily routine, such as taking a walk after dinner, cycling to work, or gardening on weekends.

REST AND RELAXATION

Rest and relaxation are important aspects of the Mediterranean lifestyle, and are closely linked to the overall health and well-being of Mediterranean people. Mediterranean cultures place a high value on relaxation and leisure time, and people often engage in activities such as reading, painting, and taking a relaxing bath.

Reduces stress: Rest and relaxation can help reduce stress by allowing the body and mind to relax and recharge.

Improves sleep: Rest and relaxation can help improve sleep by allowing the body and mind to relax and prepare for sleep.

Promotes mental well-being: Relaxation and leisure activities can help promote mental well-being by allowing the mind to focus on something other than work or stress.

Enhances creativity: Relaxation and leisure activities can also enhance creativity by allowing the mind to focus on something other than work or stress.

Improves overall quality of life: Rest and relaxation can help improve overall quality of life by allowing the body and mind to relax and recharge.

Encourages mindfulness: Mediterranean cultures place a high value on mindfulness, and activities such as yoga, meditation, and reading can help to promote mindfulness and focus on the present moment.

Enhances social connections: Relaxation and leisure activities can also enhance social connections by allowing people to spend quality time with friends and family.

Mediterranean people often take a siesta (afternoon nap) during their workdays, this practice is meant to recharge the mind and body and to give them a break from the daily routine. It's important to find activities that you enjoy and that fit into your daily routine, such as reading a book, taking a relaxing bath, or enjoying a leisurely walk. It's important to make time for rest and relaxation to ensure a balance between work and leisure and to promote overall well-being.

MINDFULNESS FOR A MEDITERRANEAN LIFESTYLE

Mindfulness is an important aspect of the Mediterranean lifestyle and is closely linked to the overall health and well-being of Mediterranean people. Mediterranean cultures place a high value on mindfulness, and people often engage in activities such as yoga, meditation, and reading to promote mindfulness and focus on the present moment.

Reduces stress: Mindfulness can help reduce stress by allowing the mind to focus on the present moment and let go of worries and anxieties.

Improves emotional well-being: Mindfulness can help improve emotional well-being by allowing the mind to focus on the present moment and let go of negative emotions.

Enhances creativity: Mindfulness can also enhance creativity by allowing the mind to focus on the present moment and let go of distractions.

Improves overall quality of life: Mindfulness can help improve overall quality of life by allowing the mind to focus on the present moment and let go of distractions.

Encourages self-awareness: Mindfulness can also encourage self-awareness by allowing people to observe their thoughts, emotions, and bodily sensations.

Enhances social connections: Mindfulness can also enhance social connections by allowing people to be more present and engaged in social interactions.

Improves physical health: Mindfulness practices such as yoga and meditation have been linked to improve physical health by reducing inflammation, lowering blood pressure and heart rate, and improving sleep.

Mediterranean people often incorporate mindfulness practices into their daily routine, they take a few minutes to focus on their breath, listen to nature, or take a moment to appreciate their surroundings. Mindfulness can be incorporated into daily activities such as cooking, walking, or even during social interactions. The key to incorporating mindfulness into your daily routine is to find activities that you enjoy and that fit into your daily routine, such as meditation, yoga, or reading. By making mindfulness a regular practice, you can improve your overall well-being and live a more balanced life.

Chapter 2
Breakfast

Spanish-Style Horchata

Prep Time: 8 minutes | Cook Time: 12 minutes | Serves 6

- 2 cups water
- 1 cup chufa seed, overnight soak
- ¼ stick cinnamon
- Zest from 1 lemon
- 2 tbsp sugar
- 4 cups cold water

1. In the pot, combine cinnamon, chufa seed and 4 cups water. Seal the lid cook on High Pressure for 1 minute. Release Pressure naturally for 10 minutes, then release the remaining Pressure quickly.
2. In a blender, add chufa seed mixture, lemon zest and sugar. Blend well to form a paste. Add 2 cups cold water into a large container. Strain the blended chufa mixture into the water. Mix well and place in the refrigerator until ready for serving. Add cinnamon stick for garnishing.

Tuna & Olive Salad

Prep Time: 5 minutes | Cook Time: 10 minutes | Serves 4

- 1½ pounds potatoes, quartered
- 2 eggs
- 3 tbsp melted butter
- Salt and pepper to taste
- 6 pickles, chopped
- 2 tbsp red wine vinegar
- ½ cup pimento stuffed green olives
- ½ cup chopped roasted red peppers
- 2 tbsp chopped fresh parsley
- 10 ounces canned tuna, drained

1. Pour 2 cups of water into the pot and add potatoes. Place a trivet over the potatoes. Lay the eggs on the trivet. Seal the lid and cook for 8 minutes on High Pressure. Do a quick release.
2. Drain and remove potatoes to a bowl. Transfer the eggs in filled with an ice water bowl. Drizzle melted butter over the potatoes and season with salt and pepper. Peel and chop the chilled eggs.
3. Add pickles, eggs, peppers, tuna, vinegar to the potatoes and mix to coat. Serve topped with olives.

Cheesy Kale Frittata

Prep Time: 10 minutes | Cook Time: 10 minutes | Serves 6

- 6 large eggs
- 2 tbsp heavy cream
- ½ tsp freshly grated nutmeg
- Salt and ground black pepper to taste
- 1½ cups kale, chopped
- ¼ cup grated Parmesan Cheese
- Cooking spray
- 1 cup water

1. In a bowl, beat eggs, nutmeg, pepper, salt, and cream until smooth. Stir in Parmesan Cheese and kale.
2. Apply a cooking spray to a cake pan. Wrap aluminum foil around outside of the pan to cover completely.
3. Place egg mixture into the prepared pan. Pour in water, set a steamer rack over the water. Gently lay the pan onto the rack. Seal the lid and cook for 10 minutes on High Pressure. Release the pressure quickly.

Breakfast Potatoes

Prep Time: 10 minutes | Cook Time: 20 minutes | Serves 6

- 1½ teaspoons olive oil, divided
- Four large potatoes, skins on, cut into cubes
- 2 teaspoons seasoned salt, divided
- 1 teaspoon minced garlic, divided
- ½ onion, diced
- Two large green peppers, cut into 1-inch chunks

1. Drizzle the Air Fryer basket with olive oil.
2. In a bowl, mix the potatoes with ½ teaspoon of oil. Sprinkle with 1 teaspoon of seasoned salt and ½ teaspoon of minced garlic. Mix to coat. Place the seasoned potatoes in the air fryer basket in a single layer. Cook for five minutes. Shake the basket and cook for another five minutes.
3. Meanwhile, stir the green peppers and onion with the remaining ½ teaspoon of oil in a bowl.
4. Sprinkle the peppers and onions with the remaining 1 teaspoon of salt and ½ teaspoon of minced garlic. Stir to coat. Add peppers and onions to the Air Fryer basket with the potatoes. Cook for five minutes. Shake the basket and cook for an additional five minutes.

Mixed Berry Muffins

Prep Time: 15 minutes | Cook Time: 15 minutes | Serves 8

- 1⅓ cups and 1 tablespoon all-purpose flour, divided
- ¼ cup granulated sugar
- 2 tablespoons brown sugar
- 2 teaspoons baking powder
- Two eggs
- ⅔ Cup whole milk
- ⅓ Cup sunflower oil
- One cup of mixed fresh berries

1. In a bowl, mix 1⅓ cups of flour, brown sugar, granulated sugar, and baking powder until mixed well.
2. In a small bowl, whisk eggs, milk, and oil until combined. Mix the egg mixture into the dry ingredients.
3. In another bowl, toss the mixed berries with the leftover 1 tablespoon of flour until coated. Stir the berries into the batter.
4. Prepare the ramekins.
5. Insert the crisper plate into the basket and then the basket into the unit. Preheat the unit (select BAKE), setting the temperature to 315°F, and set the time to 3 minutes. Select START.
6. Once the unit is preheated, place 4 ramekins into the basket and fill each three-quarter full with the batter.
7. Select BAKE, set the temperature at 315°F, and set the time for 17 minutes. Select START/STOP to begin.
8. Transfer the muffins to a wire rack to cool when the cook is done. Repeat steps with the remaining muffin cups. Let the muffins cool for ten minutes before serving.

Red Pepper and Feta Frittata

Prep Time: 10 minutes | Cook Time: 20 minutes | Serves 4

- Olive oil cooking spray
- 8 large eggs
- 1 medium red bell pepper, diced
- ½ teaspoon salt
- ½ teaspoon black pepper
- 1 garlic clove, minced
- ½ cup feta, divided

1. Preheat the air fryer to 360°F. Lightly coat the inside of a 6-inch round cake pan with olive oil cooking spray.
2. In a large bowl, beat the eggs for 1 to 2 minutes, or until well combined.
3. Add the bell pepper, salt, black pepper, and garlic to the eggs, and mix together until the bell pepper is distributed throughout.
4. Fold in ¼ cup of the feta cheese.
5. Pour the egg mixture into the prepared cake pan, and sprinkle the remaining ¼ cup of feta over the top.
6. Place into the air fryer and bake for 18 to 20 minutes, or until the eggs are set in the center.
7. Remove from the air fryer and allow to cool for 5 minutes before serving.

Pomegranate Cherry Smoothie Bowl

Prep Time: 5 minutes | Cook Time: 0 minutes | Serves 4

- 1 (16-ounce) bag frozen dark sweet cherries
- 1½ cups 2% plain Greek yogurt, plus more if needed
- ¾ cup pomegranate juice
- ⅓ cup 2% milk, plus more if needed
- 1 teaspoon vanilla extract
- ¾ teaspoon ground cinnamon
- 6 ice cubes
- ½ cup chopped pistachios
- ½ cup fresh pomegranate seeds

1. Put the cherries, yogurt, pomegranate juice, milk, vanilla, cinnamon, and ice cubes in a blender. Purée until thoroughly mixed and smooth. You'll want the mixture a little thicker than your average smoothie, but not so thick you can't pour it. If the smoothie is too thick, add another few tablespoons of milk; if it's too thin, add another few tablespoons of yogurt.
2. Pour the smoothie into four bowls. Top each with 2 tablespoons of pistachios and 2 tablespoons of pomegranate seeds, and serve immediately.

Poached Eggs on Whole Grain Avocado Toast

Prep Time: 5 minutes | Cook Time: 7 minutes | Serves 4

- Olive oil cooking spray
- 4 large eggs
- Salt
- Black pepper
- 4 pieces whole grain bread
- 1 avocado
- Red pepper flakes (optional)

1. Preheat the air fryer to 320°F. Lightly coat the inside of four small oven-safe ramekins with olive oil cooking spray.
2. Crack one egg into each ramekin, and season with salt and black pepper.
3. Place the ramekins into the air fryer basket. Close and set the timer to 7 minutes.
4. While the eggs are cooking, toast the bread in a toaster.
5. Slice the avocado in half lengthwise, remove the pit, and scoop the flesh into a small bowl. Season with salt, black pepper, and red pepper flakes, if desired. Using a fork, smash the avocado lightly.
6. Spread a quarter of the smashed avocado evenly over each slice of toast.
7. Remove the eggs from the air fryer, and gently spoon one onto each slice of avocado toast before serving.

Greek Yogurt Breakfast Parfaits with Roasted Grapes

Prep Time: 5 minutes | Cook Time: 25 minutes | Serves 4

- 1½ pounds seedless grapes (about 4 cups)
- 1 tablespoon extra-virgin olive oil
- 2 cups 2% plain Greek yogurt
- ½ cup chopped walnuts
- 4 teaspoons honey

1. Place a large, rimmed baking sheet in the oven. Preheat the oven to 450°F with the pan inside.
2. Wash the grapes and remove from the stems. Dry on a clean kitchen towel, and put in a bowl. Drizzle with the oil, and toss to coat.
3. Carefully remove the hot pan from the oven, and pour the grapes onto the pan. Bake for 20 to 23 minutes, until slightly shriveled, stirring once halfway through. Remove the baking sheet from the oven and cool on a wire rack for 5 minutes.
4. While the grapes are cooling, assemble the parfaits by spooning the yogurt into four bowls or tall glasses. Top each bowl or glass with 2 tablespoons of walnuts and 1 teaspoon of honey.
5. When the grapes are slightly cooled, top each parfait with a quarter of the grapes. Scrape any accumulated sweet grape juice onto the parfaits and serve.

Sage Soft Boiled Eggs

Prep Time: 5 minutes | Cook Time: 10 minutes | Serves 4

- 4 large eggs
- 1 cups water
- Salt and ground black pepper, to taste
- 1 tbsp sage

1. To the pressure cooker, add water and place a wire rack. Carefully place eggs on it. Seal the lid, press Steam and cook for 3 minutes on High Pressure. Do a quick release.
2. Allow to cool completely in an ice bath. Peel the eggs, in half lengthwise and season with sage, salt, and pepper before serving.

Morning Buzz Iced Coffee

Prep Time: 10 minutes | Cook Time: 0 minutes | Serves 1

- 1 cup freshly brewed strong black coffee, cooled slightly
- 1 tablespoon extra-virgin olive oil
- 1 tablespoon half-and-half or heavy cream (optional)
- 1 teaspoon MCT oil (optional)
- ⅛ teaspoon almond extract
- ⅛ teaspoon ground cinnamon

1. Pour the slightly cooled coffee into a blender or large glass (if using an immersion blender).
2. Add the olive oil, half-and-half (if using), MCT oil (if using), almond extract, and cinnamon.
3. Blend well until smooth and creamy. Drink warm and enjoy.

Orange Cardamom Buckwheat Pancakes

Prep Time: 15 minutes | Cook Time: 10 minutes | Serves 2

- ½ cup buckwheat flour
- ½ teaspoon cardamom
- ½ teaspoon baking powder
- ¼ teaspoon baking soda
- ½ cup milk
- ¼ cup plain Greek yogurt
- 1 egg
- ½ teaspoon orange extract
- 1 tablespoon maple syrup (optional)

1. In a medium bowl, combine the buckwheat flour, cardamom, baking powder, and baking soda.
2. In another bowl, combine the milk, yogurt, egg, orange extract, and maple syrup (if using) and whisk well to combine.
3. Add the wet ingredients to the dry ingredients and stir until the batter is smooth.
4. Heat a nonstick skillet or a griddle over high heat. When the pan is hot, reduce the heat to medium.
5. Pour the batter into the pan to make four 6-inch pancakes. Depending on the size of your pan, you may need to do this in four batches.

Nutty Beef Steak Salad

Prep Time: 10 minutes | Cook Time: 50 minutes | Serves 4

- 1 lb rib-eye steak, boneless
- 4 oz fresh arugula
- 1 large tomato, chopped
- ¼ cup fresh goat's cheese
- 4 almonds
- 4 walnuts
- 4 hazelnuts
- 3 tbsp olive oil
- 2 cups beef broth
- 2 tbsp red wine vinegar
- 1 tbsp Italian Seasoning mix

1. Whisk together vinegar, Italian mix, and olive oil. Brush each steak with this mixture and place in your instant pot. Pour in the broth and seal the lid.
2. Cook on Meat/Stew for 25 minutes on High Pressure. Release the Pressure naturally, for about 10 minutes, and remove the steaks along with the broth.
3. Grease the inner pot with oil and hit Sauté. Brown the steaks on both sides for 5-6 minutes. Remove from the pot and cool for 5 minutes before slicing.
4. In a bowl, mix arugula, tomato, cheese, almonds, walnuts, and hazelnuts. Top with steaks and drizzle with red wine mixture.

Mediterranean Frittata

Prep Time: 10 minutes | Cook Time: 15 minutes | Serves 2

- 4 large eggs
- 2 tablespoons fresh chopped herbs, such as rosemary, thyme, oregano, basil or 1 teaspoon dried herbs
- ¼ teaspoon salt
- Freshly ground black pepper
- 4 tablespoons extra-virgin olive oil, divided
- 1 cup fresh spinach, arugula, kale, or other leafy greens
- 4 ounces quartered artichoke hearts, rinsed, drained, and thoroughly dried
- 8 cherry tomatoes, halved
- ½ cup crumbled soft goat cheese

1. Preheat the oven to broil on low.
2. In small bowl, combine the eggs, herbs, salt, and pepper and whisk well with a fork. Set aside.
3. In a 4- to 5-inch oven-safe skillet or omelet pan, heat 2 tablespoons olive oil over medium heat. Add the spinach, artichoke hearts, and cherry tomatoes and sauté until just wilted, 1 to 2 minutes.
4. Pour in the egg mixture and let it cook undisturbed over medium heat for 3 to 4 minutes, until the eggs begin to set on the bottom.
5. Sprinkle the goat cheese across the top of the egg mixture and transfer the skillet to the oven.
6. Broil for 4 to 5 minutes, or until the frittata is firm in the center and golden brown on top.
7. Remove from the oven and run a rubber spatula around the edge to loosen the sides. Invert onto a large plate or cutting board and slice in half. Serve warm and drizzled with the remaining 2 tablespoons olive oil.

Baked Egg and Mushroom Cups

Prep Time: 5 minutes | Cook Time: 5 minutes | Serves 6

- Olive oil cooking spray
- 6 large eggs
- 1 garlic clove, minced
- ½ teaspoon salt
- ½ teaspoon black pepper
- Pinch red pepper flakes
- 8 ounces baby bella mushrooms, sliced
- 1 cup fresh baby spinach
- 2 scallions, white parts and green parts, diced

1. Preheat the air fryer to 320°F. Lightly coat the inside of six silicone muffin cups or a six-cup muffin tin with olive oil cooking spray.
2. In a large bowl, beat the eggs, garlic, salt, pepper, and red pepper flakes for 1 to 2 minutes, or until well combined.
3. Fold in the mushrooms, spinach, and scallions.
4. Divide the mixture evenly among the muffin cups.
5. Place into the air fryer and bake for 12 to 15 minutes, or until the eggs are set.
6. Remove and allow to cool for 5 minutes before serving.

Strawberry Basil Honey Ricotta Toast

Prep Time: 8 minutes | Cook Time: 2 minutes | Serves 2

- 4 slices of whole-grain bread
- ½ cup ricotta cheese (whole milk or low-fat)
- 1 tablespoon honey
- Sea salt
- 1 cup fresh strawberries, sliced
- 4 large fresh basil leaves, sliced into thin shreds

1. Toast the bread.
2. In a small bowl, combine the ricotta, honey, and a pinch or two of sea salt. Taste and add additional honey or salt if desired.
3. Spread the mixture evenly over each slice of bread (about 2 tablespoons per slice).
4. Top each piece with sliced strawberries and a few pieces of shredded basil.

Confetti Couscous

Prep Time: 5 minutes | Cook Time: 20 minutes | Serves 4-6

- 3 tablespoons extra-virgin olive oil
- 1 large onion, chopped
- 2 carrots, chopped
- 1 cup fresh peas
- ½ cup golden raisins
- 1 teaspoon salt
- 2 cups vegetable broth
- 2 cups couscous

1. In a medium pot over medium heat, gently toss the olive oil, onions, carrots, peas, and raisins together and let cook for 5 minutes.
2. Add the salt and broth, and stir to combine. Bring to a boil, and let ingredients boil for 5 minutes.
3. Add the couscous. Stir, turn the heat to low, cover, and let cook for 10 minutes. Fluff with a fork and serve

Chapter 3
Snacks & Side Dishes

Air Fried Olives

Prep Time: 10 minutes | Cook Time: 5 minutes | Serves 4

- 2 cups olives
- 2 teaspoon garlic, minced
- 2 tablespoon olive oil
- 1/2 teaspoon dried oregano
- Salt and Pepper

1. Add olives and remaining ingredients into the bowl and stir well.
2. Add to the Air Fryer basket. Set to air fry at 300°F and cook for 5 minutes.

Air Fryer Nuts

Prep Time: 10 minutes | Cook Time: 4 minutes | Serves 2

- 2 cup mixed nuts
- 1 tablespoon olive oil
- 1/4 teaspoon cayenne
- 1 teaspoon ground cumin
- 1 teaspoon pepper
- 1 teaspoon salt

1. In a bowl, add all ingredients and stir well. Add the nuts mixture to the Air Fryer basket.
2. Place a baking pan on the oven rack. Set to air fry at 350 degrees F and cook for four minutes.

Mediterranean Fruit, Veggie, and Cheese Board

Prep Time: 15 minutes | Cook Time: 0 minutes | Serves 4

- 2 cups sliced fruits, such as apples, pears, plums, or peaches
- 2 cups finger-food fruits, such as berries, cherries, grapes, or figs
- 2 cups raw vegetables cut into sticks, such as carrots, celery, broccoli, cauliflower, or whole cherry tomatoes
- 1 cup cured, canned, or jarred vegetables, such as roasted peppers or artichoke hearts, or ½ cup olives
- 1 cup cubed cheese, such as goat cheese, Gorgonzola, feta, Manchego, or Asiago (about 4 ounces)

1. Wash all the fresh produce and cut into slices or bite-size pieces, as described in the ingredients list.
2. Arrange all the ingredients on a wooden board or serving tray. Include small spoons for items like the berries and olives, and a fork or knife for the cheeses. Serve with small plates and napkins.

Lemony Garlic Hummus

Prep Time: 5 minutes | Cook Time: 0 minutes | Serves 6

- 1 (15-ounce) can chickpeas, drained, liquid reserved
- 3 tablespoons freshly squeezed lemon juice (from about 1 large lemon)
- 2 tablespoons peanut butter
- 3 tablespoons extra-virgin olive oil, divided
- 2 garlic cloves
- ¼ teaspoon kosher or sea salt (optional)
- Raw veggies or whole-grain crackers, for serving (optional)

1. In the bowl of a food processor, combine the chickpeas and 2 tablespoons of the reserved chickpea liquid with the lemon juice, peanut butter, 2 tablespoons of oil, and the garlic. Process the mixture for 1 minute. Scrape down the sides of the bowl with a rubber spatula. Process for 1 more minute, or until smooth.
2. Put in a serving bowl, drizzle with the remaining 1 tablespoon of olive oil, sprinkle with the salt, if using, and serve with veggies or crackers, if desired.

Smoky Baba Ghanoush

Prep Time: 50 minutes | Cook Time: 40 minutes | Serves 6

- 2 large eggplants, washed
- ¼ cup lemon juice
- 1 teaspoon garlic, minced
- 1 teaspoon salt
- ½ cup tahini paste
- 3 tablespoons extra-virgin olive oil

1. Grill the whole eggplants over a low flame using a gas stovetop or grill. Rotate the eggplant every 5 minutes to make sure that all sides are cooked evenly. Continue to do this for 40 minutes.
2. Remove the eggplants from the stove or grill and put them onto a plate or into a bowl; cover with plastic wrap. Let sit for 5 to 10 minutes.
3. Using your fingers, peel away and discard the charred skin of the eggplants. Cut off the stem.
4. Put the eggplants into a food processor fitted with a chopping blade. Add the lemon juice, garlic, salt, and tahini paste, and pulse the mixture 5 to 7 times.
5. Pour the eggplant mixture onto a serving plate. Drizzle with the olive oil. Serve chilled or at room temperature.

Walnut and Freekeh Pilaf

Prep Time: 15 minutes | Cook Time: 15 minutes | Serves 4

- 2½ cups freekeh
- 3 tablespoons extra-virgin olive oil, divided
- 2 medium onions, diced
- ¼ teaspoon ground cinnamon
- ¼ teaspoon ground allspice
- 5 cups chicken stock
- ½ cup chopped walnuts
- Salt
- Freshly ground black pepper
- ½ cup plain, unsweetened, full-fat Greek yogurt
- 1½ teaspoons freshly squeezed lemon juice
- ½ teaspoon garlic powder

1. In a small bowl, soak the freekeh covered in cold water for 5 minutes. Drain and rinse the freekeh, then rinse one more time.
2. In a large sauté pan or skillet, heat 2 tablespoons oil, then add the onions and cook until fragrant. Add the freekeh, cinnamon, and allspice. Stir periodically for 1 minute.
3. Add the stock and walnuts and season with salt and pepper. Bring to a simmer.
4. Cover and reduce the heat to low. Cook for 15 minutes. Once freekeh is tender, remove from the heat and allow to rest for 5 minutes.
5. In a small bowl, combine the yogurt, lemon juice, and garlic powder. You may need to add salt to bring out the flavors. Add the yogurt mixture to the freekeh and serve immediately.

Tuna Croquettes

Prep Time: 40 minutes | Cook Time: 25 minutes | Serves 36 croquettes

- 6 tablespoons extra-virgin olive oil, plus 1 to 2 cups
- 5 tablespoons almond flour, plus 1 cup, divided
- 1¼ cups heavy cream
- 1 (4-ounce) can olive oil-packed yellowfin tuna
- 1 tablespoon chopped red onion
- 2 teaspoons minced capers
- ½ teaspoon dried dill
- ¼ teaspoon freshly ground black pepper
- 2 large eggs
- 1 cup panko breadcrumbs (or a gluten-free version)

1. In a large skillet, heat 6 tablespoons olive oil over medium-low heat. Add 5 tablespoons almond flour and cook, stirring constantly, until a smooth paste forms and the flour browns slightly, 2 to 3 minutes.
2. Increase the heat to medium-high and gradually add the heavy cream, whisking constantly until completely smooth and thickened, another 4 to 5 minutes.
3. Remove from the heat and stir in the tuna, red onion, capers, dill, and pepper.
4. Transfer the mixture to an 8-inch square baking dish that is well coated with olive oil and allow to cool to room temperature. Cover and refrigerate until chilled, at least 4 hours or up to overnight.
5. To form the croquettes, set out three bowls. In one, beat together the eggs. In another, add the remaining almond flour. In the third, add the panko. Line a baking sheet with parchment paper.
6. Using a spoon, place about a tablespoon of cold prepared dough into the flour mixture and roll to coat. Shake off excess and, using your hands, roll into an oval.
7. Dip the croquette into the beaten egg, then lightly coat in panko. Set on lined baking sheet and repeat with the remaining dough.
8. In a small saucepan, heat the remaining 1 to 2 cups of olive oil, so that the oil is about 1 inch deep, over medium-high heat. The smaller the pan, the less oil you will need, but you will need more for each batch.
9. Test if the oil is ready by throwing a pinch of panko into pot. If it sizzles, the oil is ready for frying. If it sinks, it's not quite ready. Once the oil is heated, fry the croquettes 3 or 4 at a time, depending on the size of your pan, removing with a slotted spoon when golden brown. You will need to adjust the temperature of the oil occasionally to prevent burning. If the croquettes get dark brown very quickly, lower the temperature.

Easy Italian Roasted Vegetables

Prep Time: 15 minutes | Cook Time: 45 minutes | Serves 6

- Nonstick cooking spray
- 2 eggplants, peeled and sliced ⅛ inch thick
- 1 zucchini, sliced ¼ inch thick
- 1 yellow summer squash, sliced ¼ inch thick
- 2 Roma tomatoes, sliced ⅛ inch thick
- ¼ cup, plus 2 tablespoons extra-virgin olive oil, divided
- 1 tablespoon garlic powder
- ¼ teaspoon dried oregano
- ¼ teaspoon dried basil
- ¼ teaspoon salt
- Freshly ground black pepper

1. Preheat the oven to 400°F.
2. Spray a 9-by-13-inch baking dish with cooking spray. In the dish, toss the eggplant, zucchini, squash, and tomatoes with 2 tablespoons oil, garlic powder, oregano, basil, salt, and pepper.
3. Standing the vegetables up (like little soldiers), alternate layers of eggplant, zucchini, squash, and Roma tomato.
4. Drizzle the top with the remaining ¼ cup of olive oil.
5. Bake, uncovered, for 40 to 45 minutes, or until vegetables are golden brown.

Creamy Traditional Hummus

Prep Time: 5 minutes | Cook Time: 0 minutes | Serves 8

- 1 (15-ounce) can garbanzo beans, rinsed and drained
- 2 cloves garlic, peeled
- ¼ cup lemon juice
- 1 teaspoon salt
- ¼ cup plain Greek yogurt
- ½ cup tahini paste
- 2 tablespoons extra-virgin olive oil, divided

1. Add the garbanzo beans, garlic cloves, lemon juice, and salt to a food processor fitted with a chopping blade. Blend for 1 minute, until smooth.
2. Scrape down the sides of the processor. Add the Greek yogurt, tahini paste, and 1 tablespoon of olive oil and blend for another minute, until creamy and well combined.
3. Spoon the hummus into a serving bowl. Drizzle the remaining tablespoon of olive oil on top.

Garbanzo Beans with Pancetta

Prep Time: 15 minutes | Cook Time: 35 minutes | Serves 6

- 3 strips pancetta
- 1 onion, diced
- 15 oz canned garbanzo beans
- 2 cups water
- 1 cup apple cider
- 2 garlic cloves, minced
- ½ cup ketchup
- ¼ cup sugar
- 1 tsp ground mustard powder
- 1 tsp salt
- 1 tsp black pepper
- Fresh parsley to garnish

1. Cook pancetta for 5 minutes, until crispy, on Sauté mode. Add onion and garlic, and cook for 3 minutes until soft. Mix in garbanzo beans, ketchup, sugar, salt, apple cider, mustard powder, water, and pepper.
2. Seal the lid, press Bean/Chili and cook on High Pressure for 30 minutes. Release Pressure naturally for 10 minutes. Serve in bowls garnished with parsley.

Risoni with Carrots & Onion

Prep Time: 5 minutes | Cook Time: 10 minutes | Serves 6

- 1 cup orzo, rinsed
- 2 cups water
- 2 carrots, cut into sticks
- 1 large onion, chopped
- 2 tbsp olive oil
- Salt to taste
- Fresh cilantro, chopped for garnish

1. Heat oil on Sauté. Add in onion and carrots and stir-fry for about 10 minutes until tender and crispy. Remove to a plate and set aside. Add water, salt and orzo in the instant pot.
2. Seal the lid and cook on High Pressure for 1 minute. Do a quick release. Fluff the cooked orzo with a fork. Transfer to a serving plate and top with the carrots and onion. Serve scattered with cilantro.

Feta and Quinoa Stuffed Mushrooms

Prep Time: 5 minutes | Cook Time: 8 minutes | Serves 6

- 2 tablespoons finely diced red bell pepper
- 1 garlic clove, minced
- ¼ cup cooked quinoa
- ⅛ teaspoon salt
- ¼ teaspoon dried oregano
- 24 button mushrooms, stemmed
- 2 ounces crumbled feta
- 3 tablespoons whole wheat bread crumbs
- Olive oil cooking spray

1. Preheat the air fryer to 360°F.
2. In a small bowl, combine the bell pepper, garlic, quinoa, salt, and oregano.
3. Spoon the quinoa stuffing into the mushroom caps until just filled.
4. Add a small piece of feta to the top of each mushroom.
5. Sprinkle a pinch bread crumbs over the feta on each mushroom.
6. Spray the basket of the air fryer with olive oil cooking spray, then gently place the mushrooms into the basket, making sure that they don't touch each other. (Depending on the size of the air fryer, you may have to cook them in two batches.)
7. Place the basket into the air fryer and bake for 8 minutes.
8. Remove from the air fryer and serve.

Five-Ingredient Falafel with Garlic-Yogurt Sauce

Prep Time: 5 minutes | Cook Time: 15 minutes | Serves 4

- For the falafel
- 1 (15-ounce) can chickpeas, drained and rinsed
- ½ cup fresh parsley
- 2 garlic cloves, minced
- ½ tablespoon ground cumin
- 1 tablespoon whole wheat flour
- Salt
- For the garlic-yogurt sauce
- 1 cup nonfat plain Greek yogurt
- 1 garlic clove, minced
- 1 tablespoon chopped fresh dill
- 2 tablespoons lemon juice

1. Preheat the air fryer to 360°F.
2. Put the chickpeas into a food processor. Pulse until mostly chopped, then add the parsley, garlic, and cumin and pulse for another 1 to 2 minutes, or until the ingredients are combined and turning into a dough.
3. Add the flour. Pulse a few more times until combined. The dough will have texture, but the chickpeas should be pulsed into small bits.
4. Using clean hands, roll the dough into 8 balls of equal size, then pat the balls down a bit so they are about ½-thick disks.
5. Spray the basket of the air fryer with olive oil cooking spray, then place the falafel patties in the basket in a single layer, making sure they don't touch each other.
6. Fry in the air fryer for 15 minutes.
7. In a small bowl, combine the yogurt, garlic, dill, and lemon juice.
8. Once the falafel are done cooking and nicely browned on all sides, remove them from the air fryer and season with salt.
9. Serve hot with a side of dipping sauce.

Marinated Feta and Artichokes

Prep Time: 10 minutes | Cook Time: 4 hours | Serves 1.5 cups

- 4 ounces traditional Greek feta, cut into ½-inch cubes
- 4 ounces drained artichoke hearts, quartered lengthwise
- ⅓ cup extra-virgin olive oil
- Zest and juice of 1 lemon
- 2 tablespoons roughly chopped fresh rosemary
- 2 tablespoons roughly chopped fresh parsley
- ½ teaspoon black peppercorns

1. In a glass bowl or large glass jar, combine the feta and artichoke hearts. Add the olive oil, lemon zest and juice, rosemary, parsley, and peppercorns and toss gently to coat, being sure not to crumble the feta.
2. Cover and refrigerate for at least 4 hours, or up to 4 days. Pull out of the refrigerator 30 minutes before serving.

White Bean Harissa Dip

Prep Time: 10 minutes | Cook Time: 1 hour | Serves 1.5 cups

- 1 whole head of garlic
- ½ cup olive oil, divided
- 1 (15-ounce) can cannellini beans, drained and rinsed
- 1 teaspoon salt
- 1 teaspoon harissa paste (or more to taste)

1. Preheat the oven to 350°F.
2. Cut about ½ inch off the top of a whole head of garlic and lightly wrap it in foil. Drizzle 1 to 2 teaspoons of olive oil over the top of the cut side. Place it in an oven-safe dish and roast it in the oven for about 1 hour or until the cloves are soft and tender.
3. Remove the garlic from the oven and let it cool. The garlic can be roasted up to 2 days ahead of time.
4. Remove the garlic cloves from their skin and place them in the bowl of a food processor along with the beans, salt, and harissa. Purée, drizzling in as much olive oil as needed until the beans are smooth. If the dip seems too stiff, add additional olive oil to loosen the dip.
5. Taste the dip and add additional salt, harissa, or oil as needed.
6. Store in the refrigerator for up to a week.
7. Portion out ¼ cup of dip and serve with a mixture of raw vegetables and mini pita breads.

Mediterranean Trail Mix

Prep Time: 10 minutes | Cook Time: 10 minutes | Serves cups

- 1 tablespoon olive oil
- 1 tablespoon maple syrup
- 1 teaspoon vanilla
- ½ teaspoon cardamom
- ½ teaspoon allspice
- 2 cups mixed, unsalted nuts
- ¼ cup unsalted pumpkin or sunflower seeds
- ½ cup dried apricots, diced or thin sliced
- ½ cup dried figs, diced or thinly sliced
- Pinch salt

1. Combine the olive oil, maple syrup, vanilla, cardamom, and allspice in a large sauté pan over medium heat. Stir to combine.
2. Add the nuts and seeds and stir well to coat. Let the nuts and seeds toast for about 10 minutes, stirring frequently.
3. Remove from the heat, and add the dried apricots and figs. Stir everything well and season with salt.
4. Store in an airtight container.

Herby-Garlic Potatoes

Prep Time: 10 minutes | Cook Time: 20 minutes | Serves 4

- 1½ pounds potatoes
- 3 tbsp butter
- 3 cloves garlic, thinly chopped
- 2 tbsp fresh rosemary, chopped
- ½ tsp fresh thyme, chopped
- ½ tsp fresh parsley, chopped
- ¼ tsp ground black pepper
- ½ cup vegetable broth

1. Use a small knife to pierce each potato to ensure there are no blowouts when placed under pressure. Melt butter on Sauté. Add in potatoes, rosemary, parsley, pepper, thyme, and garlic, and cook for 10 minutes until potatoes are browned and the mixture is aromatic.
2. In a bowl, mix miso paste and vegetable stock. Stir in to the mixture in the instant pot. Seal the lid and cook for 5 minutes on High Pressure. Release the pressure quickly.

Chapter 4
Chicken and Poultry

Thyme Chicken with Veggies

Prep Time: 10 minutes | Cook Time: 30 minutes | Serves 4

- 4 skin-on, bone-in chicken legs
- 2 tbsp olive oil
- Salt and freshly ground black pepper to taste
- 4 cloves garlic, minced
- 1 tsp fresh chopped thyme
- ½ cup dry white wine
- 1¼ cups chicken stock
- 1 cup carrots, thinly chopped
- 1 cup parsnip, thinly chopped
- 3 tomatoes, thinly chopped
- 1 tbsp honey
- 4 slices lemon
- Fresh thyme, chopped for garnish

1. Season the chicken with pepper and salt. Warm oil on Sauté mode.
2. Arrange chicken legs into the hot oil; cook for 3 to 5 minutes each side until browned. Place in a bowl and set aside. Sauté thyme and garlic in the chicken fat for 1 minute until soft and lightly golden.
3. Add wine into the pot to deglaze, scrape the pot's bottom to get rid of any brown bits of food. Simmer the wine for 2 to 3 minutes until slightly reduced in volume.
4. Add stock, carrots, parsnips, tomatoes, pepper and salt into the pot. Lay steam rack onto veggies.
5. Into the pressure cooker's steamer basket, arrange chicken legs. Set the steamer basket onto the rack.
6. Drizzle the chicken with honey then Top with lemon slices.
7. Seal the lid and cook on High Pressure for 12 minutes. Release Pressure naturally for 10 minutes.
8. Place the chicken to a bowl. Drain the veggies and place them around the chicken. Garnish with fresh thyme leaves before serving.

Chicken with Tomatoes & Capers

Prep Time: 15 minutes | Cook Time: 30 minutes | Serves 4

- 4 chicken legs
- Sea salt and black pepper to taste
- 2 tbsp olive oil
- 1 onion, diced
- 2 garlic cloves, minced
- ⅓ cup red wine
- 2 cups diced tomatoes
- ⅓ cup capers
- ¼ cup fresh basil
- 2 pickles, chopped

1. Sprinkle pepper and salt over the chicken. Warm oil on Sauté. Add in onion and Sauté for 3 minutes until fragrant. Add in garlic and cook for 30 seconds until softened.
2. Mix the chicken with vegetables and cook for 6 to 7 minutes until lightly browned.
3. Add red wine to the pan to deglaze, scrape the pan's bottom to get rid of any browned bits of food; Stir in tomatoes. Seal the lid and cook on High Pressure for 12 minutes. Release the Pressure quickly.
4. To the chicken mixture, add basil, capers and pickles. Serve the chicken topped with the tomato sauce mixture.

Herby Chicken with Asparagus Sauce

Prep Time: 20 minutes | Cook Time: 40 minutes | Serves 4

- 1 (3 ½ pounds) Young Whole Chicken
- 4 garlic cloves, minced
- 1 tsp olive oil
- 4 fresh thyme, minced
- 3 fresh rosemary, minced
- 2 lemons, zested and quartered
- Salt and freshly ground black pepper to taste
- 2 tbsp olive oil
- 8 ounces asparagus, trimmed and chopped
- 1 onion, chopped
- 1 cup chicken stock
- 1 tbsp soy sauce
- 1 fresh thyme sprig
- Cooking spray
- 1 tbsp flour
- Chopped parsley to garnish

1. Rub all sides of the chicken with garlic, rosemary, black pepper, lemon zest, thyme, and salt. Into the chicken cavity, insert lemon wedges. Warm oil on Sauté. Add in onion and asparagus, and sauté for 5 minutes until softened. Mix chicken stock, 1 thyme sprig, black pepper, soy sauce, and salt.
2. Into the inner pot, set trivet over asparagus mixture. On top of the trivet, place the chicken with breast-side up.
3. Seal the lid, select Poultry and cook for 20 minutes on High Pressure. Do a quick release. Remove the chicken to a serving platter.
4. In the inner pot, sprinkle flour over asparagus mixture and blend the sauce with an immersion blender until desired consistency. Top the chicken with asparagus sauce and garnish with parsley.

Air-Fried Lemon and Olive Chicken

Prep Time: 10 minutes | Cook Time: 15 minutes | Serves 4

- Four Boneless Skinless Chicken Breasts
- ½ teaspoon cumin
- ½ cup butter, melted
- One lemon 1/2 juiced, 1/2 thinly sliced
- 1 cup chicken bone-broth
- 1 can pitted green olives
- ½ cup red onions, sliced
- 1 teaspoon sea salt
- ¼ teaspoon pepper

1. Season the chicken breasts with sea salt, cumin, and black pepper.
2. Preheat the Air Fryer to 370 degrees F and brush the chicken breasts with melted butter.
3. Place the breasts in a pan, and cook on your Air Fryer for about 5 minutes until evenly browned.
4. Add all remaining ingredients and cook at 320 degrees for 10 minutes.

Honey Almond-Crusted Chicken Tenders

Prep Time: 10 minutes | Cook Time: 20 minutes | Serves 4

- Nonstick cooking spray
- 1 tablespoon honey
- 1 tablespoon whole-grain or Dijon mustard
- ¼ teaspoon kosher or sea salt
- ¼ teaspoon freshly ground black pepper
- 1 pound boneless, skinless chicken breast tenders or tenderloins
- 1 cup almonds (about 3 ounces)

1. Preheat the oven to 425°F. Line a large, rimmed baking sheet with parchment paper. Place a wire cooling rack on the parchment-lined baking sheet, and coat the rack well with nonstick cooking spray.
2. In a large bowl, combine the honey, mustard, salt, and pepper. Add the chicken and stir gently to coat. Set aside.
3. Use a knife or a mini food processor to roughly chop the almonds; they should be about the size of sunflower seeds. Dump the nuts onto a large sheet of parchment paper and spread them out. Press the coated chicken tenders into the nuts until evenly coated on all sides. Place the chicken on the prepared wire rack.
4. Bake for 15 to 20 minutes, or until the internal temperature of the chicken measures 165°F on a meat thermometer and any juices run clear. Serve immediately.

Za'atar Chicken

Prep Time: 5 minutes | Cook Time: 40 minutes | Serves 4-6

- ⅓ cup plus 1 tablespoon za'atar spice
- 2 tablespoons garlic, minced
- ⅓ cup lemon juice
- ⅓ cup extra-virgin olive oil
- 1 teaspoon salt
- 8 pieces chicken thighs and drumsticks, skin on

1. Preheat the oven to 400°F.
2. In a small bowl, combine the ⅓ cup za'atar spice with the garlic, lemon juice, olive oil, and salt.
3. Place the chicken in a baking dish, and pat dry with a paper towel.
4. Pour the za'atar mixture over the chicken, making sure the pieces are completely and evenly coated.
5. Put the chicken in the oven and cook for 40 minutes.
6. Once the chicken is done cooking, sprinkle it with the remaining tablespoon of za'atar spice. Serve with potatoes, rice, or salad.

Chicken Shawarma

Prep Time: 15 minutes | Cook Time: 15 minutes | Serves 4-6

- 2 pounds boneless and skinless chicken
- ½ cup lemon juice
- ½ cup extra-virgin olive oil
- 3 tablespoons minced garlic
- 1½ teaspoons salt
- ½ teaspoon freshly ground black pepper
- ½ teaspoon ground cardamom
- ½ teaspoon cinnamon
- Hummus and pita bread, for serving (optional)

1. Cut the chicken into ¼-inch strips and put them into a large bowl.
2. In a separate bowl, whisk together the lemon juice, olive oil, garlic, salt, pepper, cardamom, and cinnamon.
3. Pour the dressing over the chicken and stir to coat all of the chicken.
4. Let the chicken sit for about 10 minutes.
5. Heat a large pan over medium-high heat and cook the chicken pieces for 12 minutes, using tongs to turn the chicken over every few minutes.
6. Serve with hummus and pita bread, if desired.

Lettuce Chicken Wraps

Prep Time: 20 minutes | Cook Time: 30 minutes | Serves 6

- 2 tbsp canola oil
- 2 pounds chicken thighs, boneless, skinless
- 1 cup pineapple juice
- ⅓ cup water
- ¼ cup soy sauce
- 2 tbsp maple syrup
- 1 tbsp rice vinegar
- 1 tsp chili-garlic sauce
- 3 tbsp cornstarch
- Salt and freshly ground black pepper to taste
- 12 large lettuce leaves
- 2 cups canned pinto beans, rinsed and drained

1. Warm oil on Sauté. In batches, sear chicken in the oil for 5 minutes until browned. Set aside in a bowl.
2. Into your pot, mix chili-garlic sauce, pineapple juice, soy sauce, vinegar, maple syrup, and water; Stir in chicken to coat. Seal the lid and cook on High Pressure for 7 minutes. Release Pressure naturally for 10 minutes. Shred the chicken with two forks. Take ¼ cup liquid from the pot to a bowl; Stir in cornstarch to dissolve.
3. Mix the cornstarch mixture with the mixture in the pot and return the chicken.
4. Select Sauté and cook for 5 minutes until the sauce thickens; add pepper and salt for seasoning.
5. Transfer beans into lettuce leaves, top with chicken carnitas and serve.

Caprese Stuffed Chicken Breasts

Prep Time: 20 minutes | Cook Time: 40 minutes | Serves 4

- 8 tablespoons extra-virgin olive oil, divided
- 2 boneless, skinless chicken breasts (about 6 ounces each)
- 4 ounces frozen spinach, thawed and drained well
- 1 cup shredded fresh mozzarella cheese
- ¼ cup chopped fresh basil
- 2 tablespoons chopped sun-dried tomatoes (preferably marinated in oil)
- 1 teaspoon salt, divided
- 1 teaspoon freshly ground black pepper, divided
- ½ teaspoon garlic powder
- 1 tablespoon balsamic vinegar

1. Preheat the oven to 375°F.
2. Drizzle 1 tablespoon olive oil in a small deep baking dish and swirl to coat the bottom.
3. Make a deep incision about 3- to 4-inches long along the length of each chicken breast to create a pocket. Using your knife or fingers, carefully increase the size of the pocket without cutting through the chicken breast. (Each breast will look like a change purse with an opening at the top.)
4. In a medium bowl, combine the spinach, mozzarella, basil, sun-dried tomatoes, 2 tablespoons olive oil, ½ teaspoon salt, ½ teaspoon pepper, and the garlic powder and combine well with a fork.
5. Stuff half of the filling mixture into the pocket of each chicken breast, stuffing down to fully fill the pocket. Press the opening together with your fingers. You can use a couple toothpicks to pin it closed if you wish.
6. In a medium skillet, heat 2 tablespoons olive oil over medium-high heat. Carefully sear the chicken breasts until browned, 3 to 4 minutes per side, being careful to not let too much filling escape. Transfer to the prepared baking dish, incision-side up. Scrape up any filling that fell out in the skillet and add it to baking dish. Cover the pan with foil and bake until the chicken is cooked through, 30 to 40 minutes, depending on the thickness of the breasts.
7. Remove from the oven and rest, covered, for 10 minutes. Meanwhile, in a small bowl, whisk together the remaining 3 tablespoons olive oil, balsamic vinegar, ½ teaspoon salt, and ½ teaspoon pepper.
8. To serve, cut each chicken breast in half, widthwise, and serve a half chicken breast drizzled with oil and vinegar.

Chicken Cacciatore

Prep Time: 20 minutes | Cook Time: 1 hour 10 minutes | Serves 4-6

- 2 tablespoons extra-virgin olive oil
- ½ cup diced carrots
- 2 garlic cloves, minced
- ½ cup chopped celery
- 2 onions, chopped
- 2 pounds chicken tenders
- 2 (14.5-ounce) cans Italian seasoned diced tomatoes, drained
- 2 cups cooked corkscrew pasta, such as whole-grain fusilli

1. In a large saucepan, heat the oil over medium-high heat and sauté the carrots, garlic, celery, and onions for about 5 minutes, until softened. Add the chicken and brown for 4 to 5 minutes on each side.
2. Add the diced tomatoes. Cover and reduce heat to simmer for an hour. Serve over pasta.

Southward Pesto Stuffed Peppers

Prep Time: 20 minutes | Cook Time: 15 minutes | Serves 4-6

- Nonstick cooking spray
- 3 large bell peppers, halved
- 2 tablespoons extra-virgin olive oil, plus more to garnish
- ¼ cup cooked chickpeas
- ½ shredded carrot
- 2 garlic cloves, minced
- 1 pound ground turkey or chicken
- Salt
- Freshly ground black pepper
- 1 cup cooked brown rice
- ½ cup halved cherry tomatoes
- ½ zucchini, chopped
- 1 tablespoon dried Italian herb medley
- 2 tablespoons chopped black olives
- 6 tablespoons prepared pesto
- ½ cup shredded Italian cheese blend

1. Preheat the oven to 350°F. Lightly spray a medium-size casserole or glass baking dish with cooking spray.
2. Bring a medium pot of water to a boil and reduce to a steady simmer. Using tongs to lower the peppers in the water, simmer each pepper half for about 3 minutes, just to soften. Remove from the water and drain in a colander.
3. In a large sauté pan or skillet, heat the olive oil over medium-high heat and sauté the chickpeas and carrot for about 5 minutes, until tender. Add the garlic and sauté for 1 minute, until fragrant. Then add the turkey, season with salt and pepper, and toss to cook evenly.
4. Just before the turkey is cooked through, add the rice, cherry tomatoes, zucchini, and herbs, and sauté an additional 5 to 7 minutes, until cooked through.
5. Remove from the heat and stir in the olives. Place the prepared pepper halves in the greased casserole dish.
6. Divide the filling evenly among the peppers. Top each pepper with 1 tablespoon of pesto and a sprinkle of Italian cheese. Bake the peppers for 7 to 10 minutes, until heated through. Allow the peppers to rest for 10 minutes before serving. Drizzle with a dash of your favorite olive oil and enjoy!

Rosemary Baked Chicken Thighs

Prep Time: 20 minutes | Cook Time: 20 minutes | Serves 4-6

- 5 tablespoons extra-virgin olive oil, divided
- 3 medium shallots, diced
- 4 garlic cloves, peeled and crushed
- 1 rosemary sprig
- 2 to 2½ pounds bone-in, skin-on chicken thighs (about 6 pieces)
- 2 teaspoons kosher salt
- ¼ teaspoon freshly ground black pepper
- 1 lemon, juiced and zested
- ⅓ cup low-sodium chicken broth

1. In a large sauté pan or skillet, heat 3 tablespoons of olive oil over medium heat. Add the shallots and garlic and cook for about a minute, until fragrant. Add the rosemary sprig.
2. Season the chicken with salt and pepper. Place it in the skillet, skin-side down, and brown for 3 to 5 minutes.
3. Once it's cooked halfway through, turn the chicken over and add lemon juice and zest.
4. Add the chicken broth, cover the pan, and continue to cook for 10 to 15 more minutes, until cooked through and juices run clear. Serve.

Greek-Style Chicken with Potatoes

Prep Time: 15 minutes | Cook Time: 25 minutes | Serves 4

- 4 potatoes, peeled and quartered
- 4 cups water
- 2 lemons, zested and juiced
- 1 tbsp olive oil
- 2 tsp fresh oregano
- Salt to taste
- ¼ tsp freshly ground black pepper
- 2 Serrano peppers, stemmed, cored, and chopped
- 4 boneless skinless chicken drumsticks
- 3 tbsp finely chopped parsley
- 1 cup packed watercress
- 1 cucumber, thinly chopped
- ½ cup cherry tomatoes, quartered
- ¼ cup Kalamata olives, pitted
- ¼ cup hummus
- ¼ cup feta cheese, crumbled
- Lemon wedges, for serving

1. In the cooker, add water and potatoes. Set trivet over them. In a baking bowl, mix lemon juice, olive oil, black pepper, oregano, zest, salt, and red pepper flakes. Add chicken drumsticks in the marinade and stir to coat.
2. Set the bowl with chicken on the trivet in the inner pot. Seal the lid, select Poultry and cook on High for 15 minutes. Do a quick release. Take out the bowl with chicken and the trivet from the pot. Drain potatoes and add parsley and salt.
3. Split the potatoes among four serving plates and top with watercress, cucumber slices, hummus, cherry tomatoes, chicken, olives, and feta cheese. Each bowl should be garnished with a lemon wedge.

Grilled Oregano Chicken Kebabs with Zucchini and Olives

Prep Time: 10 minutes | Cook Time: 20 minutes | Serves 4

- Nonstick cooking spray
- ¼ cup extra-virgin olive oil
- 2 tablespoons balsamic vinegar
- 1 teaspoon dried oregano, crushed between your fingers
- 1 pound boneless, skinless chicken breasts, cut into 1½-inch pieces
- 2 medium zucchini, cut into 1-inch pieces (about 2½ cups)
- ½ cup Kalamata olives, pitted and halved
- 2 tablespoons olive brine
- ¼ cup torn fresh basil leaves

1. Coat the cold grill with nonstick cooking spray. Heat the grill to medium-high.
2. In a small bowl, whisk together the oil, vinegar, and oregano. Divide the marinade between two large plastic zip-top bags.
3. Add the chicken to one bag and the zucchini to another. Seal and massage the marinade into both the chicken and zucchini.
4. Thread the chicken onto 6 (12-inch) wooden skewers. Thread the zucchini onto 8 or 9 (12-inch) wooden skewers. Cook the kebabs in batches on the grill for 5 minutes, flip, and grill for 5 minutes more, until any chicken juices run clear.
5. Remove the chicken and zucchini from the skewers and put in a large serving bowl. Toss with the olives, olive brine, and basil and serve.

Spanish-Seasoned Chicken and Rice

Prep Time: 15 minutes | Cook Time: 30 minutes | Serves 2

- 2 teaspoons smoked paprika
- 2 teaspoons ground cumin
- 1½ teaspoons garlic salt
- ¾ teaspoon chili powder
- ¼ teaspoon dried oregano
- 1 lemon
- 2 boneless, skinless chicken breasts
- 3 tablespoons extra-virgin olive oil, divided
- 2 large shallots, diced
- 1 cup uncooked white rice
- 2 cups vegetable stock
- 1 cup broccoli florets
- ⅓ cup chopped parsley

1. In a small bowl, whisk together the paprika, cumin, garlic salt, chili powder, and oregano. Divide in half and set aside. Into another small bowl, juice the lemon and set aside.
2. Put the chicken in a medium bowl. Coat the chicken with 2 tablespoons of olive oil and rub with half of the seasoning mix.
3. In a large pan, heat the remaining 1 tablespoon of olive oil and cook the chicken for 2 to 3 minutes on each side, until just browned but not cooked through.
4. Add shallots to the same pan and cook until translucent, then add the rice and cook for 1 more minute to toast. Add the vegetable stock, lemon juice, and the remaining seasoning mix and stir to combine. Return the chicken to the pan on top of the rice. Cover and cook for 15 minutes.
5. Uncover and add the broccoli florets. Cover and cook an additional 5 minutes, until the liquid is absorbed, rice is tender, and chicken is cooked through.
6. Top with freshly chopped parsley and serve immediately.

Lemon-Rosemary Spatchcock Chicken

Prep Time: 20 minutes | Cook Time: 45 minutes | Serves 6

- ½ cup extra-virgin olive oil, divided
- 1 (3- to 4-pound) roasting chicken
- 8 garlic cloves, roughly chopped
- 2 to 4 tablespoons chopped fresh rosemary
- 2 teaspoons salt, divided
- 1 teaspoon freshly ground black pepper, divided
- 2 lemons, thinly sliced

1. Preheat the oven to 425°F.
2. Pour 2 tablespoons olive oil in the bottom of a 9-by-13-inch baking dish or rimmed baking sheet and swirl to coat the bottom.
3. To spatchcock the bird, place the whole chicken breast-side down on a large work surface. Using a very sharp knife, cut along the backbone, starting at the tail end and working your way up to the neck. Pull apart the two sides, opening up the chicken. Flip it over, breast-side up, pressing down with your hands to flatten the bird. Transfer to the prepared baking dish.
4. Loosen the skin over the breasts and thighs by cutting a small incision and sticking one or two fingers inside to pull the skin away from the meat without removing it.
5. To prepare the filling, in a small bowl, combine ¼ cup olive oil, garlic, rosemary, 1 teaspoon salt, and ½ teaspoon pepper and whisk together.
6. Rub the garlic-herb oil evenly under the skin of each breast and each thigh. Add the lemon slices evenly to the same areas.
7. Whisk together the remaining 2 tablespoons olive oil, 1 teaspoon salt, and ½ teaspoon pepper and rub over the outside of the chicken.
8. Place in the oven, uncovered, and roast for 45 minutes, or until cooked through and golden brown. Allow to rest 5 minutes before carving to serve.

Classic Chicken Kebab

Prep Time: 30 minutes | Cook Time: 25 minutes | Serves 4

- ¼ cup olive oil
- 1 teaspoon garlic powder
- 1 teaspoon onion powder
- 1 teaspoon ground cumin
- ½ teaspoon dried oregano
- ½ teaspoon dried basil
- ¼ cup lemon juice
- 1 tablespoon apple cider vinegar
- Olive oil cooking spray
- 1 pound boneless skinless chicken thighs, cut into 1-inch pieces
- 1 red bell pepper, cut into 1-inch pieces
- 1 red onion, cut into 1-inch pieces
- 1 zucchini, cut into 1-inch pieces
- 12 cherry tomatoes

1. In a large bowl, mix together the olive oil, garlic powder, onion powder, cumin, oregano, basil, lemon juice, and apple cider vinegar.
2. Spray six skewers with olive oil cooking spray.
3. On each skewer, slide on a piece of chicken, then a piece of bell pepper, onion, zucchini, and finally a tomato and then repeat. Each skewer should have at least two pieces of each item.
4. Once all of the skewers are prepared, place them in a 9-by-13-inch baking dish and pour the olive oil marinade over the top of the skewers. Turn each skewer so that all sides of the chicken and vegetables are coated.
5. Cover the dish with plastic wrap and place it in the refrigerator for 30 minutes.
6. After 30 minutes, preheat the air fryer to 380°F. (If using a grill attachment, make sure it is inside the air fryer during preheating.)
7. Remove the skewers from the marinade and lay them in a single layer in the air fryer basket. If the air fryer has a grill attachment, you can also lay them on this instead.
8. Cook for 10 minutes. Rotate the kebabs, then cook them for 15 minutes more.
9. Remove the skewers from the air fryer and let them rest for 5 minutes before serving.

Chicken Cutlets with Greek Salsa

Prep Time: 15 minutes | Cook Time: 15 minutes | Serves 2

- 2 tablespoons olive oil, divided
- ¼ teaspoon salt, plus additional to taste
- Zest of ½ lemon
- Juice of ½ lemon
- 8 ounces chicken cutlets, or chicken breast sliced through the middle to make 2 thin pieces
- 1 cup cherry or grape tomatoes, halved or quartered (about 4 ounces)
- ½ cup minced red onion (about ⅓ medium onion)
- 1 medium cucumber, peeled, seeded and diced (about 1 cup)
- 5 to 10 pitted Greek olives, minced (more or less depending on size and your taste)
- 1 tablespoon minced fresh parsley
- 1 tablespoon minced fresh oregano
- 1 tablespoon minced fresh mint
- 1 ounce crumbled feta cheese
- 1 tablespoon red wine vinegar

1. In a medium bowl, combine 1 tablespoon of olive oil, the salt, lemon zest, and lemon juice. Add the chicken and let it marinate while you make the salsa.
2. In a small bowl, combine the tomatoes, onion, cucumber, olives, parsley, oregano, mint, feta cheese, and red wine vinegar, and toss lightly. Cover and let rest in the refrigerator for at least 30 minutes. Taste the salsa before serving and add a pinch of salt or extra herbs if desired.
3. To cook the chicken, heat the remaining 1 tablespoon of olive oil in a large nonstick skillet over medium-high heat. Add the chicken pieces and cook for 3 to 6 minutes on each side, depending on the thickness. If the chicken sticks to the pan, it's not quite ready to flip.
4. When chicken is cooked through, top with the salsa and serve.

Chapter 5
Beef, Lamb and Pork

Pork Chops & Broccoli with Gravy

Prep Time: 15 minutes | Cook Time: 30 minutes | Serves 6

- 1½ tsp salt
- 1 tsp ground black pepper
- 1 tsp garlic powder
- 1 tsp onion powder
- 1 tsp red pepper flakes
- 6 boneless pork chops
- 1 broccoli head, broken into florets
- 1 cup chicken stock
- ¼ cup butter, melted
- ¼ cup milk
- 3 tbsp flour
- ½ cup heavy cream
- Salt and ground black pepper to taste

1. Combine salt, garlic powder, flakes, onion, and black pepper. Rub the mixture onto pork chops. Place stock and broccoli in the instant pot. Lay the pork chops on top.
2. Seal the lid and cook for 15 minutes on High Pressure. Release the Pressure quickly.
3. Transfer the pork chops and broccoli to a plate. Press Sauté and simmer the liquid remaining in the pot.
4. Mix cream and flour. Pour into the simmering liquid and cook for 4 to 6 minutes until thickened and bubbly. Season with pepper and salt. Top the chops with gravy, drizzle butter over broccoli and serve.

Italian Sausage & Cannellini Stew

Prep Time: 15 minutes | Cook Time: 30 minutes | Serves 6

- 1 tbsp olive oil
- 1 pound Italian sausages, halved
- 1 celery stalk, chopped
- 1 carrot, chopped
- 1 onion, chopped
- 1 sprig fresh sage
- 1 sprig fresh rosemary
- 1 bay leaf
- 1 cup Cannellini beans, soaked and rinsed
- 2 cups vegetable stock
- 3 cups fresh spinach
- 1 tsp salt

1. Warm oil on Sauté. Add in sausage pieces and sear for 5 minutes until browned; set aside on a plate.
2. To the pot, add celery, onion, bay leaf, sage, carrot, and rosemary; cook for 3 minutes to soften slightly.
3. Stir in vegetable stock and beans. Arrange seared sausage pieces on top of the beans.
4. Seal the lid, press Bean/Chili and cook on High for 10 minutes. Release Pressure naturally for 20 minutes, do a quick release. Get rid of bay leaf, rosemary and sage. Mix spinach into the mixture to serve.

Sausage with Celeriac & Potato Mash

Prep Time: 10 minutes | Cook Time: 35 minutes | Serves 4

- 1 tbsp olive oil
- 4 pork sausages
- 1 onion
- 2 cups vegetable broth
- ½ cup water
- 4 potatoes, peeled and diced
- 1 cup celeriac, chopped
- 2 tbsp butter
- ¼ cup milk
- Salt and ground black pepper to taste
- 1 tbsp heavy cream
- 1 tsp Dijon mustard
- ½ tsp dry mustard powder
- Fresh flat-leaf parsley, chopped

1. Warm oil on Sauté mode. Add in sausages and cook for 1 to 2 minutes for each side until browned. Set the sausages to a plate. To the same pot, add onion and sauté for 3 minutes until fragrant. Press Cancel.
2. Add sausages on top of onions and pour water and broth over them. Place a trivet over onions and sausages. Put potatoes and celeriac in a steamer basket and transfer it to the trivet.
3. Seal the lid and cook for 11 minutes on High Pressure. Release the pressure quickly. Transfer potatoes and celeriac to a bowl and set sausages on a plate and cover them with aluminum foil.
4. Using a potato masher, mash potatoes and celeriac together with black pepper, milk, salt and butter until mash becomes creamy and fluffy. Adjust the seasonings.
5. Set on Sauté mode. Add the onion mixture and bring to a boil. Cook for 5 to 10 minutes until the mixture is reduced and thickened. Into the gravy, stir in dry mustard, salt, pepper, mustard and cream.
6. Place the mash in 4 bowls in equal parts, top with a sausage or two, and gravy. Garnish with parsley.

Beef & Bacon Chili

Prep Time: 15 minutes | Cook Time: 45 minutes | Serves 6

- 2 pounds stewing beef, trimmed
- 4 tsp salt,
- 4 ounces smoked bacon, cut into strips
- 1 tsp freshly ground black pepper
- 2 tsp olive oil
- 1 onion, diced
- 2 bell peppers, diced
- 3 garlic cloves, minced
- 1 tbsp ground cumin
- 1 tsp chili powder
- ½ tsp cayenne pepper
- 1 chipotle in adobo sauce, finely chopped
- 2 cups beef broth
- 29 ounces canned whole tomatoes
- 15 ounces canned kidney beans, drained

1. Set on Sauté mode and fry the bacon until crispy, about 5 minutes. Set aside.
2. Rub the beef with ½ teaspoon black pepper and 1 teaspoon salt. In the bacon fat, brown beef for 5-6 minutes; Transfer to a plate. Warm the oil. Add in garlic, peppers and onion and sauté for 3 to 4 minutes until soft. Stir in cumin, cayenne pepper, the extra pepper, salt, chipotle, chili powder and cook for 30 seconds until soft.
3. Return beef and bacon to the pot with vegetables and spices; add in tomatoes and broth. Seal the lid and cook on High Pressure for 45 minutes. Release the Pressure quickly. Stir in beans. Let simmer on Keep Warm for 10 minutes until flavors combine.

Pork Souvlaki

Prep Time: 1 hour 15 minutes | Cook Time: 10 minutes | Serves 4

- 1 (1½-pound) pork loin
- 2 tablespoons garlic, minced
- ⅓ cup extra-virgin olive oil
- ⅓ cup lemon juice
- 1 tablespoon dried oregano
- 1 teaspoon salt
- Pita bread and tzatziki, for serving (optional)

1. Cut the pork into 1-inch cubes and put them into a bowl or plastic zip-top bag.
2. In a large bowl, mix together the garlic, olive oil, lemon juice, oregano, and salt.
3. Pour the marinade over the pork and let it marinate for at least 1 hour.
4. Preheat a grill, grill pan, or lightly oiled skillet to high heat. Using wood or metal skewers, thread the pork onto the skewers.
5. Cook the skewers for 3 minutes on each side, for 12 minutes in total.
6. Serve with pita bread and tzatziki sauce, if desired.

Mediterranean Lamb Bowl

Prep Time: 15 minutes | Cook Time: 15 minutes | Serves 2

- 2 tablespoons extra-virgin olive oil
- ¼ cup diced yellow onion
- 1 pound ground lamb
- 1 teaspoon dried mint
- 1 teaspoon dried parsley
- ½ teaspoon red pepper flakes
- ¼ teaspoon garlic powder
- 1 cup cooked rice
- ½ teaspoon za'atar seasoning
- ½ cup halved cherry tomatoes
- 1 cucumber, peeled and diced
- 1 cup store-bought hummus or Garlic-Lemon Hummus
- 1 cup crumbled feta cheese
- 2 pita breads, warmed (optional)

1. In a large sauté pan or skillet, heat the olive oil over medium heat and cook the onion for about 2 minutes, until fragrant. Add the lamb and mix well, breaking up the meat as you cook. Once the lamb is halfway cooked, add mint, parsley, red pepper flakes, and garlic powder.
2. In a medium bowl, mix together the cooked rice and za'atar, then divide between individual serving bowls. Add the seasoned lamb, then top the bowls with the tomatoes, cucumber, hummus, feta, and pita (if using).

Lamb Burger

Prep Time: 15 minutes | Cook Time: 15 minutes | Serves 4

- 1 pound ground lamb
- ½ small red onion, grated
- 1 tablespoon dried parsley
- 1 teaspoon dried oregano
- 1 teaspoon ground cumin
- 1 teaspoon garlic powder
- ½ teaspoon dried mint
- ¼ teaspoon paprika
- ¼ teaspoon kosher salt
- ⅛ teaspoon freshly ground black pepper
- Extra-virgin olive oil, for panfrying
- 4 pita breads, for serving (optional)
- Tzatziki Sauce, for serving (optional)
- Pickled Onions, for serving (optional)

1. In a bowl, combine the lamb, onion, parsley, oregano, cumin, garlic powder, mint, paprika, salt, and pepper. Divide the meat into 4 small balls and work into smooth discs.
2. In a large sauté pan or skillet, heat a drizzle of olive oil over medium heat or brush a grill with oil and set it to medium. Cook the patties for 4 to 5 minutes on each side, until cooked through and juices run clear.
3. Enjoy lamb burgers in pitas, topped with tzatziki sauce and pickled onions (if using).

Spicy Lamb Burgers with Harissa Mayo

Prep Time: 15 minutes | Cook Time: 10 minutes | Serves 2

- ½ small onion, minced
- 1 garlic clove, minced
- 2 teaspoons minced fresh parsley
- 2 teaspoons minced fresh mint
- ¼ teaspoon salt
- Pinch freshly ground black pepper
- 1 teaspoon cumin
- 1 teaspoon smoked paprika
- ¼ teaspoon coriander
- 8 ounces lean ground lamb
- 2 tablespoons olive oil mayonnaise
- ½ teaspoon harissa paste (more or less to taste)
- 2 hamburger buns or pitas, fresh greens, tomato slices (optional, for serving)

1. Preheat the grill to medium-high (350–400°F) and oil the grill grate. Alternatively, you can cook these in a heavy pan (cast iron is best) on the stovetop.
2. In a large bowl, combine the onion, garlic, parsley, mint, salt, pepper, cumin, paprika, and coriander. Add the lamb and, using your hands, combine the meat with the spices so they are evenly distributed. Form meat mixture into 2 patties.
3. Grill the burgers for 4 minutes per side, or until the internal temperature registers 160°F for medium.
4. If cooking on the stovetop, heat the pan to medium-high and oil the pan. Cook the burgers for 5 to 6 minutes per side, or until the internal temperature registers 160°F.
5. While the burgers are cooking, combine the mayonnaise and harissa in a small bowl.
6. Serve the burgers with the harissa mayonnaise and slices of tomato and fresh greens on a bun or pita—or skip the bun altogether.

Beef with Garbanzo Beans

Prep Time: 10 minutes | Cook Time: 35 minutes | Serves 10

- 1 lb garbanzo beans, soaked overnight
- 1 tbsp olive oil
- 2 onions, finely chopped
- 2 ½ pounds ground beef
- 1 small jalapeño with seeds, minced
- 6 garlic cloves, minced
- ¼ cup chili powder
- 2 tbsp ground cumin
- 2 tsp salt
- 1 tsp smoked paprika
- 1 tsp dried oregano
- 1 tsp garlic powder
- ¼ tsp cayenne pepper
- 2 ½ cups beef broth
- 1 (6-ounce) can tomato puree

1. Add the beans and pour in cold water to cover 1 inch. Seal the lid and cook for 20 minutes on High Pressure. Release the pressure quickly.
2. Drain beans and rinse with cold water. Wipe clean the pot and set to Sauté mode. Warm olive oil and sauté onion for 3 minutes until soft. Add jalapeño, beef, and garlic, and stir-fry for 5 minutes until is cooked through.
3. Stir in chili powder, salt, garlic powder, paprika, cumin, oregano, and cayenne, and cook until soft, about 30 seconds. Pour in broth, beans, and tomato puree.
4. Seal the lid and cook for 20 minutes on High Pressure. Release the pressure naturally, for about 10 minutes.
5. Open the lid, press Sauté, and cook as you stir until desired consistency is attained. Spoon chili into bowls to serve.

Lamb Kofte with Yogurt Sauce

Prep Time: 30 minutes | Cook Time: 15 minutes | Serves 4

- 1 pound ground lamb
- ½ cup finely chopped fresh mint, plus 2 tablespoons
- ¼ cup almond or coconut flour
- ¼ cup finely chopped red onion
- ¼ cup toasted pine nuts
- 2 teaspoons ground cumin
- 1½ teaspoons salt, divided
- 1 teaspoon ground cinnamon
- 1 teaspoon ground ginger
- ½ teaspoon ground nutmeg
- ½ teaspoon freshly ground black pepper
- 1 cup plain whole-milk Greek yogurt
- 2 tablespoons extra-virgin olive oil
- Zest and juice of 1 lime

1. Heat the oven broiler to the low setting. You can also bake these at high heat (450 to 475°F) if you happen to have a very hot broiler. Submerge four wooden skewers in water and let soak at least 10 minutes to prevent them from burning.
2. In a large bowl, combine the lamb, ½ cup mint, almond flour, red onion, pine nuts, cumin, 1 teaspoon salt, cinnamon, ginger, nutmeg, and pepper and, using your hands, incorporate all the ingredients together well.
3. Form the mixture into 12 egg-shaped patties and let sit for 10 minutes.
4. Remove the skewers from the water, thread 3 patties onto each skewer, and place on a broiling pan or wire rack on top of a baking sheet lined with aluminum foil. Broil on the top rack until golden and cooked through, 8 to 12 minutes, flipping once halfway through cooking.
5. While the meat cooks, in a small bowl, combine the yogurt, olive oil, remaining 2 tablespoons chopped mint, remaining ½ teaspoon salt, and lime zest and juice and whisk to combine well. Keep cool until ready to use.
6. Serve the skewers with yogurt sauce.

Mediterranean Pork Chops

Prep Time: 20 minutes | Cook Time: 10 minutes | Serves 4

- ¼ cup extra-virgin olive oil
- 1 teaspoon smoked paprika
- 2 tablespoons fresh thyme leaves
- 1 teaspoon salt
- 4 pork loin chops, ½-inch-thick

1. In a small bowl, mix together the olive oil, paprika, thyme, and salt.
2. Put the pork chops in a plastic zip-top bag or a bowl and coat them with the spice mix. Let them marinate for 15 minutes.
3. Preheat a grill, grill pan, or lightly oiled skillet to high heat. Cook the pork chops for 4 minutes on each side. Serve with a Greek salad.

Beef and Goat Cheese Stuffed Peppers

Prep Time: 10 minutes | Cook Time: 30 minutes | Serves 4

- 1 pound lean ground beef
- ½ cup cooked brown rice
- 2 Roma tomatoes, diced
- 3 garlic cloves, minced
- ½ yellow onion, diced
- 2 tablespoons fresh oregano, chopped
- 1 teaspoon salt
- ½ teaspoon black pepper
- ¼ teaspoon ground allspice
- 2 bell peppers, halved and seeded
- 4 ounces goat cheese
- ¼ cup fresh parsley, chopped

1. Preheat the air fryer to 360°F.
2. In a large bowl, combine the ground beef, rice, tomatoes, garlic, onion, oregano, salt, pepper, and allspice. Mix well.
3. Divide the beef mixture equally into the halved bell peppers and top each with about 1 ounce (a quarter of the total) of the goat cheese.
4. Place the peppers into the air fryer basket in a single layer, making sure that they don't touch each other. Bake for 30 minutes.
5. Remove the peppers from the air fryer and top with fresh parsley before serving.

Beef Stew with Veggies

Prep Time: 15 minutes | Cook Time: 60 minutes | Serves 6

- ¼ cup flour
- 2 tsp salt
- 1 tsp paprika
- 1 tsp ground black pepper
- 2 pounds beef chuck, cubed
- 2 tbsp olive oil
- 2 tbsp butter
- 1 onion, diced
- 3 garlic cloves, minced
- 1 cup dry red wine
- 2 cups beef stock
- 1 tbsp dried Italian Seasoning
- 2 tsp Worcestershire sauce
- 4 cups potatoes, diced
- 2 celery stalks, chopped
- 3 cups carrots, chopped
- 3 tomatoes, chopped
- 2 bell peppers, thinly chopped
- Salt and ground black pepper to taste
- A handful of fresh parsley, chopped

1. In a bowl, mix black pepper, beef, flour, paprika, and 1 teaspoon salt. Toss the ingredients and ensure the beef is well-coated. Warm butter and oil on Sauté mode. Add in beef and cook for 8-10 minutes until browned. Set aside.
2. To the same fat, add garlic, onion, and celery, bell peppers, and cook for 4-5 minutes until tender.
3. Deglaze with wine, scrape the bottom to get rid of any browned beef bits. Pour in remaining salt, beef stock, Worcestershire sauce, and Italian seasoning.
4. Return beef to the pot; add carrots, tomatoes, and potatoes. Seal the lid, press Meat/Stew and cook on High Pressure for 35 minutes. Release Pressure naturally for 10 minutes. Taste and adjust the seasonings as necessary. Serve on plates and scatter over the parsley.

Pork Chops with Squash Purée & Mushroom Gravy

Prep Time: 10 minutes | Cook Time: 35 minutes | Serves 4

- 3 tbsp olive oil
- 2 sprigs thyme, leaves removed and chopped
- 2 sprigs rosemary, leaves removed and chopped
- 4 pork chops
- 1 cup mushrooms, chopped
- 4 cloves garlic, minced
- 1 cup chicken broth
- 1 tbsp soy sauce
- 1 pound butternut squash, cubed
- 1 tbsp olive oil
- 1 tsp cornstarch

1. Set on Sauté and heat rosemary, thyme and 2 tbsp of oil. Add the pork chops and sear for 1 minute for each side until lightly browned.
2. Sauté garlic and mushrooms in the instant pot for 5-6 minutes until mushrooms are tender. Add soy sauce and broth. Transfer pork chops to a wire trivet and place it into the pot. Over the chops, place a cake pan. Add butternut squash in the pot and drizzle with 1 tbsp olive oil.
3. Seal the lid and cook on High Pressure for 10 minutes. Release the pressure quickly. Remove the pan and trivet from the pot. Stir cornstarch into the mushroom mixture for 2 to 3 minutes until the sauce thickens.
4. Transfer the mushroom sauce to an immersion blender and blend until you attain the desired consistency. Scoop sauce into a cup with a pour spout. Smash the squash into a purée. Set pork chops on a plate and ladle squash puree next to them. Top the pork chops with gravy.

Herb-Roasted Beef Tips with Onions

Prep Time: 5 minutes | Cook Time: 10 minutes | Serves 4

- 1 pound rib eye steak, cubed
- 2 garlic cloves, minced
- 2 tablespoons olive oil
- 1 tablespoon fresh oregano
- 1 teaspoon salt
- ½ teaspoon black pepper
- 1 yellow onion, thinly sliced

1. Preheat the air fryer to 380°F.
2. In a medium bowl, combine the steak, garlic, olive oil, oregano, salt, pepper, and onion. Mix until all of the beef and onion are well coated.
3. Put the seasoned steak mixture into the air fryer basket. Roast for 5 minutes. Stir and roast for 5 minutes more.
4. Let rest for 5 minutes before serving with some favorite sides.

Slow Cooker Mediterranean Beef Stew

Prep Time: 20 minutes | Cook Time: 8 hours | Serves 2

- 1 (15-ounce) can diced or crushed tomatoes with basil
- 1 teaspoon beef base or 1 beef bouillon cube
- 2 tablespoons olive oil, divided
- 8 ounces baby bella (cremini) mushrooms, quartered
- ½ large onion, diced
- 2 garlic cloves, minced
- 1 pound cubed beef stew meat
- 3 tablespoons flour
- ¼ teaspoon salt
- Pinch freshly ground black pepper
- ¾ cup dry red wine
- ¼ cup minced brined olives
- 1 fresh rosemary sprig
- 1 (15-ounce) can white cannellini beans, drained and rinsed
- 1 medium zucchini, cut in half lengthwise and then cut into 1-inch pieces.

1. Pour the can of tomatoes into a slow cooker and set it to low heat. Add the beef base and stir to combine.
2. Heat 1 tablespoon of olive oil in a large sauté pan over medium heat. Add the mushrooms and onion and sauté for 10 minutes, or until they're golden. Add the garlic and cook for another 30 seconds. Transfer the vegetables to the slow cooker.
3. In a plastic food storage bag, combine the stew meat with the flour, salt, and pepper. Seal the bag and shake well to combine.
4. Heat the remining 1 tablespoon of oil in the sauté pan over high heat. Add the floured meat and sear to get a crust on the outside edges. Deglaze the pan by adding about half of the red wine and scraping up any browned bits on the bottom. Stir so the wine thickens a bit and transfer to the slow cooker along with any remaining wine.
5. Stir the stew to combine the ingredients. Add the olives and rosemary, cover, and cook for 6 to 8 hours on low.
6. About 30 minutes before the stew is finished, add the beans and zucchini to let them warm through.

Brisket Chili con Carne

Prep Time: 25 minutes | Cook Time: 60 minutes | Serves 6

- 1 tbsp ground black pepper
- 2 tsp salt
- 1 tsp sweet paprika
- 1 tsp cayenne pepper
- 1 tsp chili powder
- ½ tsp garlic salt
- ½ tsp onion powder
- 1 (4 pounds) beef brisket
- 1 cup beef broth
- 2 bay leaves
- 2 tbsp Worcestershire sauce
- 14 ounces canned black beans, drained and rinsed

1. In a bowl, combine pepper, paprika, chili powder, cayenne pepper, salt, onion powder and garlic salt; rub onto brisket pieces to coat.
2. Add the brisket to your instant pot. Cover with Worcestershire sauce and water.
3. Seal the lid and cook on High Pressure for 50 minutes. Release the pressure naturally for 10 minutes.
4. Transfer the brisket to a cutting board. Drain any liquid present in the pot using a fine-mesh strainer; get rid of any solids and fat.
5. Slice brisket, arrange the slices onto a platter, add the black beans on side and spoon the cooking liquid over the slices and beans to serve.

Beef and Pumpkin Stew

Prep Time: 10 minutes | Cook Time: 25 minutes | Serves 6

- 2 tbsp canola oil
- 2 pounds stew beef, cut into 1-inch chunks
- 1 cup red wine
- 1 onion, chopped
- 1 tsp garlic powder
- 1 tsp salt
- 3 whole cloves
- 1 bay leaf
- 3 carrots, chopped
- ½ butternut pumpkin, chopped
- 2 tbsp cornstarch
- 3 tbsp water

1. Warm oil on Sauté mode. Brown the beef for 5 minutes on each side.
2. Deglaze the pot with wine, scrape the bottom to get rid of any browned beef bits. Add in onion, salt, bay leaf, cloves, and garlic powder. Seal the lid, press Meat/Stew and cook on High for 15 minutes.
3. Release the Pressure quickly. Add in pumpkin and carrots without stirring.
4. Seal the lid and cook on High Pressure for 5 minutes. Release the Pressure quickly.
5. In a bowl, mix water and cornstarch until cornstarch dissolves completely; mix into the stew. Allow the stew to simmer while uncovered on Keep Warm for 5 minutes until you attain the desired thickness.

Chapter 6
Fish and Seafood

Steamed Mediterranean Cod

Prep Time: 5 minutes | Cook Time: 15 minutes | Serves 4

- 1 pound cherry tomatoes, halved
- 1 bunch fresh thyme sprigs
- 4 fillets cod
- 1 tsp olive oil
- 1 clove garlic, pressed
- 3 pinches salt
- 2 cups water
- 1 cup white rice
- 1 cup Kalamata olives
- 2 tbsp pickled capers
- 1 tbsp olive oil
- 1 pinch ground black pepper

1. Line a parchment paper on the basket of your instant pot. Place about half the tomatoes in a single layer on the paper. Sprinkle with thyme, reserving some for garnish.
2. Arrange cod fillets on top. Sprinkle with a little bit of olive oil.
3. Spread the garlic, pepper, salt, and remaining tomatoes over the fish. In the pot, mix rice and water.
4. Lay a trivet over the rice and water. Lower steamer basket onto the trivet.
5. Seal the lid, and cook for 7 minutes on Low Pressure. Release the Pressure quickly.
6. Remove the steamer basket and trivet from the pot. Use a fork to fluff rice.
7. Plate the fish fillets and apply a garnish of olives, reserved thyme, pepper, remaining olive oil, and capers. Serve with rice.

Steamed Sea Bass with Turnips

Prep Time: 5 minutes | Cook Time: 10 minutes | Serves 4

- 1½ cups water
- 1 lemon, sliced
- 4 sea bass fillets
- 4 sprigs thyme
- 1 white onion, cut into thin rings
- 2 turnips, chopped
- 2 pinches salt
- 1 pinch ground black pepper
- 2 tsp olive oil

1. Add water and set a rack into the pot.
2. Line a parchment paper to the bottom of the steamer basket. Place lemon slices in a single layer on the rack.
3. Arrange fillets on the top of the lemons, cover with onion and thyme sprigs. Top with turnip slices.
4. Drizzle pepper, salt, and olive oil over the mixture. Put steamer basket onto the rack.
5. Seal lid and cook on Low pressure for 8 minutes. Release the pressure quickly.
6. Serve over the delicate onion rings and thinly turnips.

Spanish Chorizo & Shrimp Boil

Prep Time: 10 minutes | Cook Time: 20 minutes | Serves 4

- 3 red potatoes
- 3 ears corn, cut into rounds
- 2 cups water
- 1 cup white wine
- 4 Spanish chorizo, sliced
- 1 pound shrimp, peeled and deveined
- 2 tbsp seafood seasoning
- Salt to taste
- 1 lemon, cut into wedges
- ¼ cup butter, melted

1. Add all ingredients, except butter and lemon wedges. Do not stir.
2. Seal the lid and cook for 2 minutes on High Pressure. Release the pressure quickly.
3. Drain the mixture through a colander. Transfer to a serving platter. Serve with melted butter and lemon wedges.

Cod in Lemon Sweet Sauce

Prep Time: 10 minutes | Cook Time: 10 minutes | Serves 3

- 1 lb cod fillets, skinless and boneless
- 1 cup maple syrup
- ½ cup soy sauce
- 3 garlic cloves, finely chopped
- 1 lemon, juiced
- 1 tsp black pepper, ground
- 1 tsp sea salt
- 1 tbsp butter

1. In a bowl, mix maple syrup, soy sauce, garlic, lemon juice, pepper, and salt. Stir until combined and set aside. Grease the pot with butter. Place the fillets at the bottom and pour over the maple sauce.
2. Seal the lid and cook on Steam for 8 minutes on High. Release the pressure naturally, for about 5 minutes.

Air Fried Fish Fillet

Prep Time: 10 minutes | Cook Time: 20 minutes | Serves 2

- 12 oz. white fish fillets
- 1/2 tsp. lemon pepper seasoning
- 1/2 tsp. garlic powder
- 1/2 tsp. onion powder
- Salt and Pepper

1. Spray the Air Fryer basket with cook spray.
2. Season the fish fillets with onion powder, lemon pepper seasoning, garlic powder, pepper, and salt.
3. Place parchment paper in the bottom of the Air Fryer basket and the fish fillets on top.
4. Set the Air Fryer to "air fry" at 350° F and cook for 10 minutes.

Speedy Tilapia with Red Onion and Avocado

Prep Time: 10 minutes | Cook Time: 5 minutes | Serves 4

- 1 tablespoon extra-virgin olive oil
- 1 tablespoon freshly squeezed orange juice
- ¼ teaspoon kosher or sea salt
- 4 (4-ounce) tilapia fillets, more oblong than square, skin-on or skinned
- ¼ cup chopped red onion (about ⅛ onion)
- 1 avocado, pitted, skinned, and sliced

1. In a 9-inch glass pie dish, use a fork to mix together the oil, orange juice, and salt. Working with one fillet at a time, place each in the pie dish and turn to coat on all sides. Arrange the fillets in a wagon-wheel formation, so that one end of each fillet is in the center of the dish and the other end is temporarily draped over the edge of the dish. Top each fillet with 1 tablespoon of onion, then fold the end of the fillet that's hanging over the edge in half over the onion. When finished, you should have 4 folded-over fillets with the fold against the outer edge of the dish and the ends all in the center.
2. Cover the dish with plastic wrap, leaving a small part open at the edge to vent the steam. Microwave on high for about 3 minutes. The fish is done when it just begins to separate into flakes (chunks) when pressed gently with a fork.
3. Top the fillets with the avocado and serve.

Air Fry Catfish

Prep Time: 5 minutes | Cook Time: 13 minutes | Serves 4

- 1 tbsp. chopped parsley
- 1 tbsp. olive oil
- ¼ C. seasoned fish fry
- 4 catfish fillets

1. Preheat your Air Fryer to 400 degrees F.
2. Rinse off catfish fillets and pat dry. Add fish fry seasoning and then catfish to a Ziploc bag. Shake the bag and ensure the fish gets well coated. Spray each fillet with olive oil.
3. Add fillets to the Air Fryer basket. Set the temperature to 400°F and the time to 10 minutes.
4. Cook for 10 minutes. Then flip and cook another 2-3 minutes.

Grilled Fish on Lemons

Prep Time: 10 minutes | Cook Time: 10 minutes | Serves 4

- 4 (4-ounce) fish fillets, such as tilapia, salmon, catfish, cod, or your favorite fish
- Nonstick cooking spray
- 3 to 4 medium lemons
- 1 tablespoon extra-virgin olive oil
- ¼ teaspoon freshly ground black pepper
- ¼ teaspoon kosher or sea salt

1. Using paper towels, pat the fillets dry and let stand at room temperature for 10 minutes. Meanwhile, coat the cold cooking grate of the grill with nonstick cooking spray, and preheat the grill to 400°F, or medium-high heat. Or preheat a grill pan over medium-high heat on the stove top.
2. Cut one lemon in half and set half aside. Slice the remaining half of that lemon and the remaining lemons into ¼-inch-thick slices. (You should have about 12 to 16 lemon slices.) Into a small bowl, squeeze 1 tablespoon of juice out of the reserved lemon half.
3. Add the oil to the bowl with the lemon juice, and mix well. Brush both sides of the fish with the oil mixture, and sprinkle evenly with pepper and salt.
4. Carefully place the lemon slices on the grill (or the grill pan), arranging 3 to 4 slices together in the shape of a fish fillet, and repeat with the remaining slices. Place the fish fillets directly on top of the lemon slices, and grill with the lid closed. (If you're grilling on the stove top, cover with a large pot lid or aluminum foil.) Turn the fish halfway through the cooking time only if the fillets are more than half an inch thick. (See tip for cooking time.) The fish is done and ready to serve when it just begins to separate into flakes (chunks) when pressed gently with a fork.

Mediterranean Grilled Shrimp

Prep Time: 20 minutes | Cook Time: 5 minutes | Serves 4

- 2 tablespoons garlic, minced
- ½ cup lemon juice
- 3 tablespoons fresh Italian parsley, finely chopped
- ¼ cup extra-virgin olive oil
- 1 teaspoon salt
- 2 pounds jumbo shrimp (21-25), peeled and deveined

1. In a large bowl, mix the garlic, lemon juice, parsley, olive oil, and salt.
2. Add the shrimp to the bowl and toss to make sure all the pieces are coated with the marinade. Let the shrimp sit for 15 minutes.
3. Preheat a grill, grill pan, or lightly oiled skillet to high heat. While heating, thread about 5 to 6 pieces of shrimp onto each skewer.
4. Place the skewers on the grill, grill pan, or skillet and cook for 2 to 3 minutes on each side until cooked through. Serve warm.

Garlicky Shrimp with Mushrooms
Prep Time: 10 minutes | Cook Time: 15 minutes | Serves 4

- 1 pound peeled and deveined fresh shrimp
- 1 teaspoon salt
- 1 cup extra-virgin olive oil
- 8 large garlic cloves, thinly sliced
- ½ teaspoon red pepper flakes
- ¼ cup chopped fresh flat-leaf Italian parsley
- Zucchini Noodles or Riced Cauliflower, for serving

1. Rinse the shrimp and pat dry. Place in a small bowl and sprinkle with the salt.
2. In a large rimmed, thick skillet, heat the olive oil over medium-low heat. Add the garlic and heat until very fragrant, 3 to 4 minutes, reducing the heat if the garlic starts to burn.
3. Add the mushrooms and sauté for 5 minutes, until softened. Add the shrimp and red pepper flakes and sauté until the shrimp begins to turn pink, another 3 to 4 minutes.
4. Remove from the heat and stir in the parsley. Serve over Zucchini Noodles or Riced Cauliflower.

Basil-Parmesan Crusted Salmon
Prep Time: 5 minutes | Cook Time: 15 minutes | Serves 4

- Grated Parmesan: 3 tablespoons
- Skinless four salmon fillets
- Salt: 1/4 teaspoon
- Freshly ground black pepper
- Low-fat mayonnaise: 3 tablespoons
- Basil leaves, chopped
- Half lemon

1. Let the Air Fryer preheat to 400 °F. Spray the basket with olive oil.
2. Season the salmon with pepper, salt, and lemon juice.
3. Mix two tablespoons of Parmesan cheese in a bowl with mayonnaise and basil leaves.
4. Add this mix and the rest of the Parmesan on top of the salmon and cook for seven minutes.

Air Fryer Lemon Cod
Prep Time: 5 minutes | Cook Time: 10 minutes | Serves 1

- One cod fillet
- Dried parsley
- Salt and pepper to taste
- Garlic powder
- One lemon

1. In a bowl, mix all ingredients and coat the fish fillet with spices.
2. Slice the lemon and lay it at the bottom of the Air Fryer basket. Put spiced fish on top. Cover the fish with lemon slices.
3. Cook for ten minutes at 375 °F, until the internal temperature of the fish should be 145 °F.

Salmon with Dill Chutney
Prep Time: 10 minutes | Cook Time: 5 minutes | Serves 2

- 2 salmon fillets
- Juice from ½ lemon
- ¼ tsp paprika
- Salt and freshly ground pepper to taste
- 2 cups water
- For Chutney:
- ¼ cup fresh dill
- Juice from ½ lemon
- Sea salt to taste
- ¼ cup extra virgin olive oil

1. In a food processor, blend all the chutney ingredients until creamy. Set aside.
2. To your cooker, add the water and place a steamer basket.
3. Arrange salmon fillets skin-side down on the steamer basket. Drizzle lemon juice over salmon and sprinkle with paprika. Seal the lid and cook for 3 minutes on High Pressure. Release the pressure quickly.
4. Season the fillets with pepper and salt, Transfer to a serving plate and top with the dill chutney.

Garlic-Cilantro Shrimp
Prep Time: 20 minutes | Cook Time: 10 minutes | Serves 4

- ⅓ cup lemon juice
- 4 garlic cloves
- 1 cup fresh cilantro leaves
- ½ teaspoon ground coriander
- 3 tablespoons extra-virgin olive oil
- 1 teaspoon salt
- 1½ pounds large shrimp (21-25), deveined and shells removed

1. In a food processor, pulse the lemon juice, garlic, cilantro, coriander, olive oil, and salt 10 times.
2. Put the shrimp in a bowl or plastic zip-top bag, pour in the cilantro marinade, and let sit for 15 minutes.
3. Preheat a skillet on high heat.
4. Put the shrimp and marinade in the skillet. Cook the shrimp for 3 minutes on each side. Serve warm.

Shrimp over Black Bean Linguine

Prep Time: 10 minutes | Cook Time: 15 minutes | Serves 4

- 1 pound black bean linguine or spaghetti
- 1 pound fresh shrimp, peeled and deveined
- 4 tablespoons extra-virgin olive oil
- 1 onion, finely chopped
- 3 garlic cloves, minced
- ¼ cup basil, cut into strips

1. Bring a large pot of water to a boil and cook the pasta according to the package instructions.
2. In the last 5 minutes of cooking the pasta, add the shrimp to the hot water and allow them to cook for 3 to 5 minutes. Once they turn pink, take them out of the hot water, and, if you think you may have overcooked them, run them under cool water. Set aside.
3. Reserve 1 cup of the pasta cooking water and drain the noodles. In the same pan, heat the oil over medium-high heat and cook the onion and garlic for 7 to 10 minutes. Once the onion is translucent, add the pasta back in and toss well.
4. Plate the pasta, then top with shrimp and garnish with basil.

Easy Shrimp and Orzo Salad

Prep Time: 10 minutes | Cook Time: 10 minutes | Serves 4

- 1 cup orzo
- 1 hothouse cucumber, seeded and chopped
- ½ cup finely diced red onion
- 2 tablespoons extra-virgin olive oil
- 2 pounds (16- to 18-count) shrimp, peeled and deveined
- 3 lemons, juiced
- Salt
- Freshly ground black pepper
- ¾ cup crumbled feta cheese
- 2 tablespoons dried dill
- 1 cup chopped fresh flat-leaf parsley

1. Bring a large pot of water to a boil, then add the orzo. Cover, reduce heat, and simmer for 15 to 18 minutes, until the orzo is tender. Drain in a colander and set aside to cool.
2. In a separate bowl, combine the cucumber and red onion and set aside.
3. In a medium pan, heat the olive oil over medium heat. Add the shrimp. Reduce the heat and cook for 2 minutes on each side, or until fully cooked and pink.
4. Add the cooked shrimp to the bowl with the cucumber and onion, along with the lemon juice, and toss. Season with salt and pepper. Top with feta and dill, toss gently, and finish with parsley.

Pesto Shrimp with Wild Rice Pilaf

Prep Time: 5 minutes | Cook Time: 5 minutes | Serves 4

- 1 pound medium shrimp, peeled and deveined
- ¼ cup pesto sauce
- 1 lemon, sliced
- 2 cups cooked wild rice pilaf

1. Preheat the air fryer to 360°F.
2. In a medium bowl, toss the shrimp with the pesto sauce until well coated.
3. Place the shrimp in a single layer in the air fryer basket. Put the lemon slices over the shrimp and roast for 5 minutes.
4. Remove the lemons and discard. Serve a quarter of the shrimp over ½ cup wild rice with some favorite steamed vegetables.

Chapter 7
Vegetarian Recipes

Green Minestrone

Prep Time: 10 minutes | Cook Time: 20 minutes | Serves 4

- 2 tbsp olive oil
- 1 head broccoli, cut into florets
- 4 celery stalks, chopped thinly
- 1 leek, chopped thinly
- 1 zucchini, chopped
- 1 cup green beans
- 2 cups vegetable broth
- 3 whole black peppercorns
- water to cover
- 2 cups chopped kale

1. Add broccoli, leek, beans, salt, peppercorns, zucchini, and celery. Mix in vegetable broth, oil, and water. Seal the lid and cook on High Pressure for 4 minutes. Release pressure naturally for 5 minutes, then release the remaining pressure quickly. Stir in kale; set on Sauté, and cook until tender.

Vegan Carrot Gazpacho

Prep Time: 10 minutes | Cook Time: 25 minutes plus 2 hours to chill | Serves 4

- 1 pound trimmed carrots
- 1 pound tomatoes, chopped
- 1 cucumber, peeled and chopped
- ¼ cup olive oil
- 2 tbsp lemon juice
- 1 red onion, chopped
- 2 cloves garlic
- 2 tbsp white wine vinegar
- Salt and freshly ground black pepper to taste

1. Add carrots, salt and enough water. Seal the lid and cook for 20 minutes on High Pressure. Do a quick release. Set the beets to a bowl and place in the refrigerator to cool. In a blender, add carrots, cucumber, red onion, pepper, garlic, oil, tomatoes, lemon juice, vinegar, and salt. Blend until very smooth. Place gazpacho to a serving bowl, chill while covered for 2 hours.

Baked Egg Tomato

Prep Time: 5 minutes | Cook Time: 30 minutes | Serves 2

- Two large fresh tomatoes
- Two eggs
- Salt and Pepper

1. Cut the top of the tomato and spoon out the tomato innards.
2. Break the egg into each tomato. Place tomatoes on a baking pan.
3. Select bake mode and set the oven to 350 degrees F for thirty mins, then place the pan into the Air Fryer.
4. Season with salt and pepper. Garnish with parsley.

Garlic Veggie Mash with Parmesan

Prep Time: 5 minutes | Cook Time: 10 minutes | Serves 6

- 3 pounds Yukon Gold potatoes, chopped
- 1½ cups cauliflower, broken into florets
- 1 carrot, chopped
- 1 cup Parmesan Cheese, shredded
- ¼ cup butter, melted
- ¼ cup milk
- 1 tsp salt
- 1 garlic clove, minced
- Fresh parsley for garnish

1. Into the pot, add veggies, salt and cover with enough water. Seal the lid and cook on High Pressure for 10 minutes. Release the pressure quickly. Drain the vegetables and mash them with a potato masher.
2. Add garlic, butter and milk, and Whisk until everything is well incorporated. Serve topped with Parmesan cheese and chopped parsley.

Steamed Broccoli

Prep Time: 10 minutes | Cook Time: 3 minutes | Serves 2

- 1 pound broccoli florets
- 1 teaspoon olive oil
- 1½ cups water
- Salt and pepper

1. Add water to the bottom of the Air Fryer and set the basket on top.
2. Stir the broccoli florets with pepper, salt, and oil until evenly combined. Then transfer to the basket.
3. Cook at 350° F for five minutes.

Baked Macaroni with Cheese

Prep Time: 10 minutes | Cook Time: 25 minutes | Serves 4

- 1 pound elbow macaroni
- ½ pound Cheddar cheese, shredded
- Two eggs
- Four tablespoons butter
- One teaspoon Dijon mustard
- 12 oz. evaporated milk
- ½ c. breadcrumbs
- Salt and pepper

1. Cook macaroni according to package directions.
2. Meanwhile, spray a baking dish with cook spray.
3. Add all ingredients except bread crumbs to the dish and stir well to combine. Sprinkle with bread crumbs.
4. Cover with foil and place the pan on the rack. Bake at 350° F for 15-20 minutes.
5. Remove the foil, and cook for another 5 minutes.

Pesto Arborio Rice Bowls with Veggies

Prep Time: 10 minutes | Cook Time: 20 minutes | Serves 2

- 1 cup arborio rice, rinsed
- 2 cups water
- salt and ground black pepper to taste
- 1 small beet, peeled and cubed
- 1 cup broccoli florets
- 1 carrot, peeled and chopped
- ½ pound Brussels sprouts
- 2 eggs
- ¼ cup pesto sauce
- lemon wedges, for serving

1. In the pot, mix water, salt, rice and pepper. Set trivet over rice and set steamer basket on top. To the steamer basket, add eggs, Brussels sprouts, broccoli, beet cubes, carrots, pepper and salt.
2. Seal the lid and cook for 1 minute on High Pressure. Release pressure naturally for 10 minutes, then release any remaining pressure quickly. Remove steamer basket and trivet from the pot and set the eggs to a bowl of ice water. Peel and halve the eggs. Use a fork to fluff the rice.
3. Separate rice, broccoli, carrots, beet, Brussels sprouts, eggs, and a dollop of pesto into two bowls. Serve alongside a lemon wedge.

Garlicky Broccoli Rabe with Artichokes

Prep Time: 5 minutes | Cook Time: 10 minutes | Serves 4

- 2 pounds fresh broccoli rabe
- ½ cup extra-virgin olive oil, divided
- 3 garlic cloves, finely minced
- 1 teaspoon salt
- 1 teaspoon red pepper flakes
- 1 (13.75-ounce) can artichoke hearts, drained and quartered
- 1 tablespoon water
- 2 tablespoons red wine vinegar
- Freshly ground black pepper

1. Trim away any thick lower stems and yellow leaves from the broccoli rabe and discard. Cut into individual florets with a couple inches of thin stem attached.
2. In a large skillet, heat ¼ cup olive oil over medium-high heat. Add the trimmed broccoli, garlic, salt, and red pepper flakes and sauté for 5 minutes, until the broccoli begins to soften. Add the artichoke hearts and sauté for another 2 minutes.
3. Add the water and reduce the heat to low. Cover and simmer until the broccoli stems are tender, 3 to 5 minutes.
4. In a small bowl, whisk together remaining ¼ cup olive oil and the vinegar. Drizzle over the broccoli and artichokes. Season with ground black pepper, if desired.

Quinoa with Almonds and Cranberries

Prep Time: 15 minutes | Cook Time: 0 minutes | Serves 4

- 2 cups cooked quinoa
- ⅓ teaspoon cranberries or currants
- ¼ cup sliced almonds
- 2 garlic cloves, minced
- 1¼ teaspoons salt
- ½ teaspoon ground cumin
- ½ teaspoon turmeric
- ¼ teaspoon ground cinnamon
- ¼ teaspoon freshly ground black pepper

1. In a large bowl, toss the quinoa, cranberries, almonds, garlic, salt, cumin, turmeric, cinnamon, and pepper and stir to combine.
2. Enjoy alone or with roasted cauliflower

Greek Stuffed Collard Greens

Prep Time: 10 minutes | Cook Time: 20 minutes | Serves 4

- 1 (28-ounce) can low-sodium or no-salt-added crushed tomatoes
- 8 collard green leaves (about ⅓ pound), tough tips of stems cut off
- 1 recipe Mediterranean Lentils and Rice or 2 (10-ounce) bags frozen grain medley (about 4 cups), cooked
- 2 tablespoons grated Parmesan cheese

1. Preheat the oven to 400°F. Pour the tomatoes into a baking pan and set aside.
2. Fill a large stockpot about three-quarters of the way with water and bring to a boil. Add the collard greens and cook for 2 minutes. Drain in a colander. Put the greens on a clean towel or paper towels and blot dry.
3. To assemble the stuffed collards, lay one leaf flat on the counter vertically. Add about ½ cup of the lentils and rice mixture to the middle of the leaf, and spread it evenly along the middle of the leaf. Fold one long side of the leaf over the rice filling, then fold over the other long side so it is slightly overlapping. Take the bottom end, where the stem was, and gently but firmly roll up until you have a slightly square package. Carefully transfer the stuffed leaf to the baking pan, and place it seam-side down in the crushed tomatoes. Repeat with the remaining leaves.
4. Sprinkle the leaves with the grated cheese, and cover the pan with aluminum foil. Bake for 20 minutes, or until the collards are tender-firm, and serve. (If you prefer softer greens, bake for an additional 10 minutes.)

Walnut Pesto Zoodles

Prep Time: 15 minutes | Cook Time: 10 minutes | Serves 4

- 4 medium zucchini (makes about 8 cups of zoodles)
- ¼ cup extra-virgin olive oil, divided
- 2 garlic cloves, minced (about 1 teaspoon), divided
- ½ teaspoon crushed red pepper
- ¼ teaspoon freshly ground black pepper, divided
- ¼ teaspoon kosher or sea salt, divided
- 2 tablespoons grated Parmesan cheese, divided
- 1 cup packed fresh basil leaves
- ¾ cup walnut pieces, divided

1. Make the zucchini noodles (zoodles) using a spiralizer or your vegetable peeler to make ribbons (run the peeler down the zucchini to make long strips). In a large bowl, gently mix to combine the zoodles with 1 tablespoon of oil, 1 minced garlic clove, all the crushed red pepper, ⅛ teaspoon of black pepper, and ⅛ teaspoon of salt. Set aside.
2. In a large skillet over medium-high heat, heat ½ tablespoon of oil. Add half of the zoodles to the pan and cook for 5 minutes, stirring every minute or so. Pour the cooked zoodles into a large serving bowl, and repeat with another ½ tablespoon of oil and the remaining zoodles. Add those zoodles to the serving bowl when they are done cooking.
3. While the zoodles are cooking, make the pesto. If you're using a food processor, add the remaining minced garlic clove, ⅛ teaspoon of black pepper, and ⅛ teaspoon of salt, 1 tablespoon of Parmesan, all the basil leaves, and ¼ cup of walnuts. Turn on the processor, and slowly drizzle the remaining 2 tablespoons of oil into the opening until the pesto is completely blended. If you're using a high-powered blender, add the 2 tablespoons of oil first and then the rest of the pesto ingredients. Pulse until the pesto is completely blended.
4. Add the pesto to the zoodles along with the remaining 1 tablespoon of Parmesan and the remaining ½ cup of walnuts. Mix together well and serve.

Mediterranean Cauliflower Tabbouleh

Prep Time: 15 minutes plus 30 minutes to chill | Cook Time: 5 minutes | Serves 6

- 6 tablespoons extra-virgin olive oil, divided
- 4 cups Riced Cauliflower
- 3 garlic cloves, finely minced
- 1½ teaspoons salt
- ½ teaspoon freshly ground black pepper
- ½ large cucumber, peeled, seeded, and chopped
- ½ cup chopped mint leaves
- ½ cup chopped Italian parsley
- ½ cup chopped pitted Kalamata olives
- 2 tablespoons minced red onion
- Juice of 1 lemon (about 2 tablespoons)
- 2 cups baby arugula or spinach leaves
- 2 medium avocados, peeled, pitted, and diced
- 1 cup quartered cherry tomatoes

1. In a large skillet, heat 2 tablespoons of olive oil over medium-high heat. Add the riced cauliflower, garlic, salt, and pepper and sauté until just tender but not mushy, 3 to 4 minutes. Remove from the heat and place in a large bowl.
2. Add the cucumber, mint, parsley, olives, red onion, lemon juice, and remaining 4 tablespoons olive oil and toss well. Place in the refrigerator, uncovered, and refrigerate for at least 30 minutes, or up to 2 hours.
3. Before serving, add the arugula, avocado, and tomatoes and toss to combine well. Season to taste with salt and pepper and serve cold or at room temperature.

Green Beans with Feta & Nuts

Prep Time: 7 minutes | Cook Time: 8 minutes | Serves 6

- Juice from 1 lemon
- 1½ cups water
- 2 pounds green beans, trimmed
- 1 cup chopped toasted pine nuts
- 1 cup feta cheese, crumbled
- 6 tbsp olive oil
- ½ tsp salt
- Black pepper to taste

1. Add water and set the rack over the water and the steamer basket on the rack. Loosely heap green beans into the steamer basket. Seal lid and cook on High Pressure for 5 minutes.
2. Release pressure quickly. Drop green beans into a salad bowl. Top with the olive oil, feta cheese, pepper, and pine nuts.

Mediterranean Veggie Bowl

Prep Time: 10 minutes | Cook Time: 20 minutes | Serves 4

- 2 cups water
- 1 cup of either bulgur wheat #3 or quinoa, rinsed
- 1½ teaspoons salt, divided
- 1 pint (2 cups) cherry tomatoes, cut in half
- 1 large bell pepper, chopped
- 1 large cucumber, chopped
- 1 cup Kalamata olives
- ½ cup freshly squeezed lemon juice
- 1 cup extra-virgin olive oil
- ½ teaspoon freshly ground black pepper

1. In a medium pot over medium heat, boil the water. Add the bulgur (or quinoa) and 1 teaspoon of salt. Cover and cook for 15 to 20 minutes.
2. To arrange the veggies in your 4 bowls, visually divide each bowl into 5 sections. Place the cooked bulgur in one section. Follow with the tomatoes, bell pepper, cucumbers, and olives.
3. In a small bowl, whisk together the lemon juice, olive oil, remaining ½ teaspoon salt, and black pepper.
4. Evenly spoon the dressing over the 4 bowls.
5. Serve immediately or cover and refrigerate for later.

Grilled Veggie and Hummus Wrap

Prep Time: 15 minutes | Cook Time: 10 minutes | Serves 6

- 1 large eggplant
- 1 large onion
- ½ cup extra-virgin olive oil
- 1 teaspoon salt
- 6 lavash wraps or large pita bread
- 1 cup Creamy Traditional Hummus

1. Preheat a grill, large grill pan, or lightly oiled large skillet on medium heat.
2. Slice the eggplant and onion into circles. Brush the vegetables with olive oil and sprinkle with salt.
3. Cook the vegetables on both sides, about 3 to 4 minutes each side.
4. To make the wrap, lay the lavash or pita flat. Spread about 2 tablespoons of hummus on the wrap.
5. Evenly divide the vegetables among the wraps, layering them along one side of the wrap. Gently fold over the side of the wrap with the vegetables, tucking them in and making a tight wrap.
6. Lay the wrap seam side-down and cut in half or thirds.
7. You can also wrap each sandwich with plastic wrap to help it hold its shape and eat it later.

Rustic Vegetable and Brown Rice Bowl

Prep Time: 15 minutes | Cook Time: 20 minutes | Serves 4

- Nonstick cooking spray
- 2 cups broccoli florets
- 2 cups cauliflower florets
- 1 (15-ounce) can chickpeas, drained and rinsed
- 1 cup carrots sliced 1 inch thick
- 2 to 3 tablespoons extra-virgin olive oil, divided
- Salt
- Freshly ground black pepper
- 2 to 3 tablespoons sesame seeds, for garnish
- 2 cups cooked brown rice
- 3 to 4 tablespoons tahini
- 2 tablespoons honey
- 1 lemon, juiced
- 1 garlic clove, minced
- Salt
- Freshly ground black pepper

1. Preheat the oven to 400°F. Spray two baking sheets with cooking spray.
2. Cover the first baking sheet with the broccoli and cauliflower and the second with the chickpeas and carrots. Toss each sheet with half of the oil and season with salt and pepper before placing in oven.
3. Cook the carrots and chickpeas for 10 minutes, leaving the carrots still just crisp, and the broccoli and cauliflower for 20 minutes, until tender. Stir each halfway through cooking.
4. To make the dressing, in a small bowl, mix the tahini, honey, lemon juice, and garlic. Season with salt and pepper and set aside.
5. Divide the rice into individual bowls, then layer with vegetables and drizzle dressing over the dish.

Rosemary-Roasted Red Potatoes

Prep Time: 5 minutes | Cook Time: 20 minutes | Serves 6

- 1 pound red potatoes, quartered
- ¼ cup olive oil
- ½ teaspoon kosher salt
- ¼ teaspoon black pepper
- 1 garlic clove, minced
- 4 rosemary sprigs

1. Preheat the air fryer to 360°F.
2. In a large bowl, toss the potatoes with the olive oil, salt, pepper, and garlic until well coated.
3. Pour the potatoes into the air fryer basket and top with the sprigs of rosemary.
4. Roast for 10 minutes, then stir or toss the potatoes and roast for 10 minutes more.
5. Remove the rosemary sprigs and serve the potatoes. Season with additional salt and pepper, if needed.

Chapter 8
Desserts and Staples

Cinnamon Apple Crisp

Prep Time: 10 minutes | Cook Time: 20 minutes | Serves 5

- Topping
- ½ cup oat flour
- ½ cup old-fashioned rolled oats
- ½ cup granulated sugar
- ¼ cup olive oil
- Filling
- 5 apples, peeled, cored, and halved
- 2 tbsp arrowroot powder
- ½ cup water
- 1 tsp ground cinnamon
- ¼ tsp ground nutmeg
- ½ tsp vanilla paste

1. In a bowl, combine sugar, oat flour, rolled oats, and olive oil to form coarse crumbs. Ladle the apples into the instant pot. Mix water with arrowroot powder in a bowl. Stir in salt, nutmeg, cinnamon, and vanilla.
2. Toss in the apples to coat. Apply oat topping to the apples. Seal the lid and cook on High Pressure for 10 minutes. Release the pressure naturally for 5 minutes, then release the remaining Pressure quickly.

Dark Chocolate Brownies

Prep Time: 10 minutes | Cook Time: 30 minutes | Serves 6

- 1 ½ cups water
- 2 eggs
- ⅓ cup granulated sugar
- ¼ cup olive oil
- ⅓ cup flour
- ⅓ cup cocoa powder
- ⅓ cup dark chocolate chips
- ⅓ cup chopped Walnuts
- 1 tbsp milk
- ½ tsp baking powder
- 1 tbsp vanilla extract
- A pinch salt

1. Add water and set steamer rack into the cooker. Line a parchment paper on the steamer basket. In a bowl, beat eggs and sugar to mix until smooth. Stir in oil, cocoa, milk, salt baking powder, chocolate chips, flour, walnuts, vanilla, and sea salt. Transfer the batter to the prepared steamer basket.
2. Arrange into an even layer. Seal the lid, press Cake and cook for 20 minutes on High Pressure. Release the pressure quickly. Let brownie cool before cutting. Use powdered sugar to dust and serve.

Cinnamon Pumpkin Pudding

Prep Time: 10 minutes | Cook Time: 10 minutes | Serves 4

- 1 lb pumpkin, peeled and chopped into bite-sized pieces
- 1 cup granulated sugar
- ½ cup cornstarch
- 4 cups apple juice, unsweetened
- 1 tsp cinnamon, ground
- 3-4 cloves

1. In a bowl, combine sugar and apple juice until sugar dissolves completely.
2. Pour the mixture into the pot and stir in cornstarch, cinnamon, cloves, and pumpkin. Seal the lid, and cook for 10 minutes on High Pressure. Do a quick release. Pour in the pudding into 4 serving bowls. Let cool to room temperature and refrigerate overnight.

Chilled Dark Chocolate Fruit Kebabs

Prep Time: 20 minutes | Cook Time: 20 minutes | Serves 6

- 12 strawberries, hulled
- 12 cherries, pitted
- 24 seedless red or green grapes
- 24 blueberries
- 8 ounces dark chocolate

1. Line a large, rimmed baking sheet with parchment paper. On your work surface, lay out six 12-inch wooden skewers.
2. Thread the fruit onto the skewers, following this pattern: 1 strawberry, 1 cherry, 2 grapes, 2 blueberries, 1 strawberry, 1 cherry, 2 grapes, and 2 blueberries (or vary according to taste!). Place the kebabs on the prepared baking sheet.
3. In a medium, microwave-safe bowl, heat the chocolate in the microwave for 1 minute on high. Stir until the chocolate is completely melted.
4. Spoon the melted chocolate into a small plastic sandwich bag. Twist the bag closed right above the chocolate, and snip the corner of the bag off with scissors. Squeeze the bag to drizzle lines of chocolate over the kebabs.
5. Place the sheet in the freezer and chill for 20 minutes before serving.

Minty Watermelon Salad

Prep Time: 10 minutes | Cook Time: 0 minutes | Serves 6

- 1 medium watermelon
- 1 cup fresh blueberries
- 2 tablespoons fresh mint leaves
- 2 tablespoons lemon juice
- ⅓ cup honey

1. Cut the watermelon into 1-inch cubes. Put them in a bowl.
2. Evenly distribute the blueberries over the watermelon.
3. Finely chop the mint leaves and put them into a separate bowl.
4. Add the lemon juice and honey to the mint and whisk together.
5. Drizzle the mint dressing over the watermelon and blueberries. Serve cold.

Baklava

Prep Time: 10 minutes | Cook Time: 40 minutes | Serves 12

- 1½ cups finely chopped walnuts
- 1 teaspoon ground cinnamon
- ¼ teaspoon ground cardamom (optional)
- 1 cup water
- ½ cup sugar
- ½ cup honey
- 2 tablespoons freshly squeezed lemon juice
- 1 cup salted butter, melted
- 20 large sheets phyllo pastry dough, at room temperature

1. Preheat the oven to 350°F.
2. In a small bowl, gently mix the walnuts, cinnamon, and cardamom (if using) and set aside.
3. In a small pot, bring the water, sugar, honey, and lemon juice just to a boil. Remove from the heat.
4. Put the butter in a small bowl. Onto an ungreased 9-by-13-inch baking sheet, put 1 layer of phyllo dough and slowly brush with butter. Be careful not to tear the phyllo sheets as you butter them. Carefully layer 1 or 2 more phyllo sheets, brushing each with butter in the baking pan, and then layer ⅛ of the nut mix; layer 2 sheets and add another ⅛ of the nut mix; repeat with 2 sheets and nuts until you run out of nuts and dough, topping with the remaining phyllo dough sheets.
5. Slice 4 lines into the baklava lengthwise and make another 4 or 5 slices diagonally across the pan.
6. Put in the oven and cook for 30 to 40 minutes, or until golden brown.
7. Remove the baklava from the oven and immediately cover it with the syrup.

Creamy Grapefruit-Tarragon Dressing

Prep Time: 5 minutes | Cook Time: 0 minutes | Serves 4

- ½ cup avocado oil mayonnaise or Homemade Aioli
- 2 tablespoons Dijon mustard
- 1 teaspoon dried tarragon or 1 tablespoon chopped fresh tarragon
- Zest and juice of ½ grapefruit (about 2 tablespoons juice)
- ½ teaspoon salt
- ¼ teaspoon freshly ground black pepper
- 1 to 2 tablespoons water (optional)

1. In a large mason jar or glass measuring cup, combine the mayonnaise, Dijon, tarragon, grapefruit zest and juice, salt, and pepper and whisk well with a fork until smooth and creamy. If a thinner dressing is preferred, thin out with water.

Nutmeg Squash Tart

Prep Time: 5 minutes | Cook Time: 25 minutes | Serves 8

- 15 oz mashed squash
- 6 fl oz milk
- ½ tsp cinnamon, ground
- ½ tsp nutmeg
- ½ tsp salt
- 3 large eggs
- ½ cup granulated sugar
- 1 pack pate brisee

1. Place squash puree in a large bowl. Add milk, cinnamon, eggs, nutmeg, salt, and sugar. Whisk together until well incorporated. Grease a baking dish with oil.
2. Gently place pate brisee creating the edges with hands. Pour the squash mixture over and flatten the surface with a spatula. Pour 1 cup of water in the pot and insert the trivet. Lower the baking dish on the trivet.
3. Seal the lid, and cook for 25 minutes on High Pressure. Do a quick release. Transfer the pie to a serving platter. Refrigerate overnight before serving.

Homemade Sweet Potato Chips

Prep Time: 5 minutes | Cook Time: 15 minutes | Serves 2

- 1 large sweet potato, sliced thin
- ⅛ teaspoon salt
- 2 tablespoons olive oil

1. Preheat the air fryer to 380°F.
2. In a small bowl, toss the sweet potatoes, salt, and olive oil together until the potatoes are well coated.
3. Put the sweet potato slices into the air fryer and spread them out in a single layer.
4. Fry for 10 minutes. Stir, then air fry for 3 to 5 minutes more, or until the chips reach the preferred level of crispiness.

Chocolate Pudding

Prep Time: 10 minutes plus 1 hour to chill | **Cook Time:** 0 minutes | **Serves 4**

- 2 ripe avocados, halved and pitted
- ¼ cup unsweetened cocoa powder
- ¼ cup heavy whipping cream, plus more if needed
- 2 teaspoons vanilla extract
- 1 to 2 teaspoons liquid stevia or monk fruit extract (optional)
- ½ teaspoon ground cinnamon (optional)
- ¼ teaspoon salt
- Whipped cream, for serving (optional)

1. Using a spoon, scoop out the ripe avocado into a blender or large bowl, if using an immersion blender. Mash well with a fork.
2. Add the cocoa powder, heavy whipping cream, vanilla, sweetener (if using), cinnamon (if using), and salt. Blend well until smooth and creamy, adding additional cream, 1 tablespoon at a time, if the mixture is too thick.
3. Cover and refrigerate for at least 1 hour before serving. Serve chilled with additional whipped cream, if desired.

Flan with Whipping Cream

Prep Time: 10 minutes | **Cook Time:** 20 minutes | **Serves 4**

- ½ cup granulated sugar
- 4 tbsp. caramel syrup
- 1 cup water
- 3 eggs
- ½ tsp vanilla extract
- ½ tbsp milk
- 5 oz whipping cream

1. Combine milk, whipping cream and vanilla extract in your instant pot. Press Sauté, and cook for 5 minutes, or until small bubbles form. Set aside.
2. Using an electric mixer, whisk the eggs and sugar. Gradually add the cream mixture and whisk until well combined. Divide the caramel syrup between 4 ramekins. Fill with egg mixture and place them on top of the trivet. Pour in water.
3. Seal the lid, and cook for 15 minutes on High Pressure. Do a quick release. remove the ramekins from the pot and cool completely before serving.

Arugula and Walnut Pesto

Prep Time: 5 minutes | **Cook Time:** 0 minutes | **Serves 8**

- 6 cups packed arugula
- 1 cup chopped walnuts
- ½ cup shredded Parmesan cheese
- 2 garlic cloves, peeled
- ½ teaspoon salt
- 1 cup extra-virgin olive oil

1. In a food processor, combine the arugula, walnuts, cheese, and garlic and process until very finely chopped. Add the salt. With the processor running, stream in the olive oil until well blended.
2. If the mixture seems too thick, add warm water, 1 tablespoon at a time, until smooth and creamy. Store in a sealed container in the refrigerator.

Lemon Cookies

Prep Time: 10 minutes | **Cook Time:** 10 minutes | **Serves 12 cookies**

- Nonstick cooking spray
- ¾ cup granulated sugar
- ½ cup butter
- 1½ teaspoons vinegar
- 1 large egg
- 1 teaspoon grated lemon zest
- 1¾ cup flour
- 1 teaspoon baking powder
- ¼ teaspoon baking soda
- ¾ cup confectioners' sugar
- ¼ cup freshly squeezed lemon juice
- 1 teaspoon finely grated lemon zest

1. Preheat the oven to 350°F. Spray a baking sheet with cooking spray and set aside.
2. In a medium bowl, cream the sugar and butter. Next, stir in the vinegar, and then add the egg and lemon zest, and mix well. Sift the flour, baking powder, and baking soda into the bowl and mix until combined.
3. Spoon the mixture onto a prepared baking sheet in 12 equal heaps. Bake for 10 to 12 minutes. Be sure not to burn the bottoms.
4. While the cookies are baking, make the lemon glaze in a small bowl by mixing the sugar, lemon juice, and lemon zest together.
5. Remove the cookies from the oven and brush with lemon glaze.

Flourless Chocolate Brownies with Raspberry Balsamic Sauce

Prep Time: 10 minutes | Cook Time: 20 minutes | Serves 2

- For the raspberry sauce
- ¼ cup good-quality balsamic vinegar
- 1 cup frozen raspberries
- For the brownie
- ½ cup black beans with no added salt, rinsed
- 1 large egg
- 1 tablespoon olive oil
- ½ teaspoon vanilla extract
- 4 tablespoons unsweetened cocoa powder
- ¼ cup sugar
- ¼ teaspoon baking powder
- Pinch salt
- ¼ cup dark chocolate chips

1. Combine the balsamic vinegar and raspberries in a saucepan and bring the mixture to a boil. Reduce the heat to medium and let the sauce simmer for 15 minutes, or until reduced to ½ cup. If desired, strain the seeds and set the sauce aside until the brownie is ready.
2. Preheat the oven to 350°F and set the rack to the middle position. Grease two 8-ounce ramekins and place them on a baking sheet.
3. In a food processor, combine the black beans, egg, olive oil, and vanilla. Purée the mixture for 1 to 2 minutes, or until it's smooth and the beans are completely broken down. Scrape down the sides of the bowl a few times to make sure everything is well-incorporated.
4. Add the cocoa powder, sugar, baking powder, and salt and purée again to combine the dry ingredients, scraping down the sides of the bowl as needed.
5. Stir the chocolate chips into the batter by hand. Reserve a few if you like, to sprinkle over the top of the brownies when they come out of the oven.
6. Pour the brownies into the prepared ramekins and bake for 15 minutes, or until firm. The center will look slightly undercooked. If you prefer a firmer brownie, leave it in the oven for another 5 minutes, or until a toothpick inserted in the middle comes out clean.
7. Remove the brownies from the oven. If desired, sprinkle any remaining chocolate chips over the top and let them melt into the warm brownies.
8. Let the brownies cool for a few minutes and top with warm raspberry sauce to serve.

Dark Chocolate and Cranberry Granola Bars

Prep Time: 5 minutes | Cook Time: 15 minutes | Serves 6

- 2 cups certified gluten-free quick oats
- 2 tablespoons sugar-free dark chocolate chunks
- 2 tablespoons unsweetened dried cranberries
- 3 tablespoons unsweetened shredded coconut
- ½ cup raw honey
- 1 teaspoon ground cinnamon
- ⅛ teaspoon salt
- 2 tablespoons olive oil

1. Preheat the air fryer to 360°F. Line an 8-by-8-inch baking dish with parchment paper that comes up the side so you can lift it out after cooking.
2. In a large bowl, mix together all of the ingredients until well combined.
3. Press the oat mixture into the pan in an even layer.
4. Place the pan into the air fryer basket and bake for 15 minutes.
5. Remove the pan from the air fryer, and lift the granola cake out of the pan using the edges of the parchment paper.
6. Allow to cool for 5 minutes before slicing into 6 equal bars.
7. Serve immediately, or wrap in plastic wrap and store at room temperature for up to 1 week.

Spiced Baked Pears with Mascarpone

Prep Time: 10 minutes | Cook Time: 20 minutes | Serves 2

- 2 ripe pears, peeled
- 1 tablespoon plus 2 teaspoons honey, divided
- 1 teaspoon vanilla, divided
- ¼ teaspoon ginger
- ¼ teaspoon ground coriander
- ¼ cup minced walnuts
- ¼ cup mascarpone cheese
- Pinch salt

1. Preheat the oven to 350°F and set the rack to the middle position. Grease a small baking dish.
2. Cut the pears in half lengthwise. Using a spoon, scoop out the core from each piece. Place the pears with the cut side up in the baking dish.
3. Combine 1 tablespoon of honey, ½ teaspoon of vanilla, ginger, and coriander in a small bowl. Pour this mixture evenly over the pear halves.
4. Sprinkle walnuts over the pear halves.
5. Bake for 20 minutes, or until the pears are golden and you're able to pierce them easily with a knife.
6. While the pears are baking, mix the mascarpone cheese with the remaining 2 teaspoons honey, ½ teaspoon of vanilla, and a pinch of salt. Stir well to combine.
7. Divide the mascarpone among the warm pear halves and serve.

Appendix 1 Measurement Conversion Chart

Volume Equivalents (Dry)

US STANDARD	METRIC (APPROXIMATE)
1/8 teaspoon	0.5 mL
1/4 teaspoon	1 mL
1/2 teaspoon	2 mL
3/4 teaspoon	4 mL
1 teaspoon	5 mL
1 tablespoon	15 mL
1/4 cup	59 mL
1/2 cup	118 mL
3/4 cup	177 mL
1 cup	235 mL
2 cups	475 mL
3 cups	700 mL
4 cups	1 L

Volume Equivalents (Liquid)

US STANDARD	US STANDARD (OUNCES)	METRIC (APPROXIMATE)
2 tablespoons	1 fl.oz.	30 mL
1/4 cup	2 fl.oz.	60 mL
1/2 cup	4 fl.oz.	120 mL
1 cup	8 fl.oz.	240 mL
1 1/2 cup	12 fl.oz.	355 mL
2 cups or 1 pint	16 fl.oz.	475 mL
4 cups or 1 quart	32 fl.oz.	1 L
1 gallon	128 fl.oz.	4 L

Temperatures Equivalents

FAHRENHEIT(F)	CELSIUS(C) APPROXIMATE
225 °F	107 °C
250 °F	120 ° °C
275 °F	135 °C
300 °F	150 °C
325 °F	160 °C
350 °F	180 °C
375 °F	190 °C
400 °F	205 °C
425 °F	220 °C
450 °F	235 °C
475 °F	245 °C
500 °F	260 °C

Weight Equivalents

US STANDARD	METRIC (APPROXIMATE)
1 ounce	28 g
2 ounces	57 g
5 ounces	142 g
10 ounces	284 g
15 ounces	425 g
16 ounces (1 pound)	455 g
1.5 pounds	680 g
2 pounds	907 g

Appendix 2 The Dirty Dozen and Clean Fifteen

The Environmental Working Group (EWG) is a nonprofit, nonpartisan organization dedicated to protecting human health and the environment Its mission is to empower people to live healthier lives in a healthier environment. This organization publishes an annual list of the twelve kinds of produce, in sequence, that have the highest amount of pesticide residue-the Dirty Dozen-as well as a list of the fifteen kinds ofproduce that have the least amount of pesticide residue-the Clean Fifteen.

THE DIRTY DOZEN	
The 2016 Dirty Dozen includes the following produce. These are considered among the year's most important produce to buy organic:	
Strawberries	Spinach
Apples	Tomatoes
Nectarines	Bell peppers
Peaches	Cherry tomatoes
Celery	Cucumbers
Grapes	Kale/collard greens
Cherries	Hot peppers

The Dirty Dozen list contains two additional itemskale/collard greens and hot peppers-because they tend to contain trace levels of highly hazardous pesticides.

THE CLEAN FIFTEEN	
The least critical to buy organically are the Clean Fifteen list. The following are on the 2016 list:	
Avocados	Papayas
Corn	Kiw
Pineapples	Eggplant
Cabbage	Honeydew
Sweet peas	Grapefruit
Onions	Cantaloupe
Asparagus	Cauliflower
Mangos	

Some of the sweet corn sold in the United States are made from genetically engineered (GE) seedstock. Buy organic varieties of these crops to avoid GE produce.

Appendix 3 Index

RHONDA M. REEVES

Printed in Great Britain
by Amazon

23845714R00044